Meet
Smarter

A Guide to *Better* Nonprofit Board Meetings

By Outi Flynn

BOARDSOURCE
Building Effective Nonprofit Boards

Formerly the National Center for Nonprofit Boards

Library of Congress Cataloging-in-Publication Data

Flynn, Outi.

   Meet smarter: a guide to better nonprofit board meetings / by Outi
Flynn.

     p. cm.
   Includes bibliographical references and index.
   ISBN 1-58686-079-8 (pbk.)
  1. Corporate meetings--Handbooks, manuals, etc. 2. Business meetings--
Handbooks, manuals, etc. 3. Boards of directors--Handbooks, manuals, etc. 4. Chief
executive officers--Handbooks, manuals, etc. 5. Parliamentary practice--Handbooks,
manuals, etc. 6. Nonprofit organizations--Management--Handbooks, manuals, etc. I.
Title: Nonprofit board meetings. II. Title.

   HD2743.F57 2004
   658.4'56--dc22

  2004011635

Published by BoardSource
1828 L Street, NW, Suite 900
Washington, DC 20036

BoardSource, formerly the National Center for Nonprofit Boards, is the premier resource for practical information, tools and best practices, training, and leadership development for board members of nonprofit organizations worldwide. Through our highly acclaimed programs and services, BoardSource enables organizations to fulfill their missions by helping build strong and effective nonprofit boards.

BoardSource provides assistance and resources to nonprofit leaders through workshops, training, and our extensive Web site, www.boardsource.org. A team of BoardSource governance consultants works directly with nonprofit leaders to design specialized solutions to meet organizations' needs and assists nongovernmental organizations around the world through partnerships and capacity building. As the world's largest, most comprehensive publisher of materials on nonprofit governance, BoardSource offers a wide selection of books, videotapes, and CDs. BoardSource also hosts the BoardSource Leadership Forum, bringing together approximately 800 governance experts, board members, and chief executives of nonprofit organizations from around the world.

Created out of the nonprofit sector's critical need for governance guidance and expertise, BoardSource is a 501(c)(3) nonprofit organization that has provided practical solutions to nonprofit organizations of all sizes in diverse communities. In 2001, BoardSource changed its name from the National Center for Nonprofit Boards to better reflect its mission. Today, BoardSource has more than 15,000 members and has served more than 75,000 nonprofit leaders.

For more information, please visit our Web site, www.boardsource.org, e-mail us at mail@boardsource.org, or call us at 800-883-6262.

Have You Used These BoardSource Resources?

VIDEOS

Meeting the Challenge: An Orientation to Nonprofit Board Service

Speaking of Money: A Guide to Fund-Raising for Nonprofit Board Members

BOOKS

The Board Chair Handbook

Managing Conflicts of Interest: Practical Guidelines for Nonprofit Boards

Driving Strategic Planning: A Nonprofit Executive's Guide

The Board-Savvy CEO: How To Build a Strong, Positive Relationship with Your Board

Presenting: Board Orientation

Presenting: Nonprofit Financials

The Board Meeting Rescue Kit: 20 Ideas for Jumpstarting Your Board Meetings

The Board Building Cycle: Nine Steps to Finding, Recruiting, and Engaging Nonprofit Board Members

The Policy Sampler: A Resource for Nonprofit Boards

To Go Forward, Retreat! The Board Retreat Handbook

Nonprofit Board Answer Book: Practical Guide for Board Members and Chief Executives

Nonprofit Board Answer Book II: Beyond the Basics

The Legal Obligations of Nonprofit Boards

Self-Assessment for Nonprofit Governing Boards

Assessment of the Chief Executive

Fearless Fundraising

The Nonprofit Board's Guide to Bylaws

Understanding Nonprofit Financial Statements

Transforming Board Structure: New Possibilities for Committees and Task Forces

THE GOVERNANCE SERIES

1. *Ten Basic Responsibilities of Nonprofit Boards*

2. *Financial Responsibilities of Nonprofit Boards*

3. *Structures and Practices of Nonprofit Boards*

4. *Fundraising Responsibilities of Nonprofit Boards*

5. *Legal Responsibilities of Nonprofit Boards*

6. *The Nonprofit Board's Role in Setting and Advancing the Mission*

7. *The Nonprofit Board's Role in Planning and Evaluation*

8. *How To Help Your Board Govern More and Manage Less*

9. *Leadership Roles in Nonprofit Governance*

For an up-to-date list of publications and information about current prices, membership, and other services, please call BoardSource at 800-883-6262 or visit our Web site at www.boardsource.org.

Contents

LIST OF BOXES

INDEX OF APPROPRIATE AUDIENCE

All are strongly encouraged to read the text in its entirety. However, for those who intend to focus solely on their specific role in meetings as chief executive, board chair, board member, or staff member, please refer to the following list for the most appropriate sections for reference.

Chief Executive

Chapter 1

Introduction

Peruse the shelves of a well-stocked bookstore, and it is quickly evident that there is a rather respectable array of books on how to run meetings. While these books may tend to focus on parliamentary order, logistical problems, or the mechanics of meetings, few address the fundamental problems inherent to board meetings: relationships, group dynamics, and how to work well together. It is ironic that meeting problems tend to be at the heart of so many malfunctioning boards and there are so few helpful references that cover these issues. After all, the boardroom is the "cradle" where the board shapes governance issues and decides on the future of its nonprofit.

It is difficult to write a guide for productive board meetings because the main challenge is not just about the logistics of conducting meetings, but one of personal dynamics. For years, BoardSource has addressed thousands of questions dealing with boring and unproductive meetings. Questions range from how to get members to attend meetings to finding tools to train the chair as an effective facilitator. Some look for solutions to eliminating interminable sessions or improving minute taking. Others ask whether the chief executive should be present at executive sessions or who may invite outsiders to the meeting.

It is evident that the lack of efficient communication and relationship building create the majority of the dilemmas, but some structure and form — however a specific board defines them — can improve the setting that invites more productive interaction. The legal stipulations for board meetings also cannot be ignored. It is important to understand all the elements that help a group of people, charged with a major mission, turn the time they spend together into an enjoyable and fruitful effort.

Chapter 1 of this book examines the guidelines the law dictates to nonprofit boards. It discusses the general principles behind Sunshine Laws and outlines what the organization's bylaws should say about board meetings. Even if the law sets the acceptable parameters, using common sense, good practices, and ethical standards helps everyone involved turn meetings into effective forums for advancing the objectives of the organization.

Chapter 2 focuses on thorough preparation as the key to laying the foundation for bringing board members together. This chapter presents the how, when, and where of planning a board meeting. The chief executive and the chair may be the brains behind a successful board meeting, but without the endless and often thankless blood, sweat, and tears of the staff in arranging the details and logistics, good intentions can turn into sour grapes. Productive meeting planning takes intellectual capital as well as thoughtful organization.

A board is at its best when it communicates effectively, both during and in between meetings. But in the spirit of good communication, board members may often be flooded with documents to read: meeting minutes, agendas, meeting reports, etc. Without these reporting mechanisms, however, there is no permanent record of what the board discussed or decided upon. Chapter 3 addresses the content of a variety of board documents, the value of a consent agenda, and the legal protections documentation provides the board.

Chapter 4 looks at the process of how boards structure their meetings, make decisions, and vote. The text provides alternatives to using strict parliamentary order and discusses a variety of decision-making methods.

Chapter 5 introduces the players and participants who must be present or who have the power to influence the outcome of a meeting. There is no meeting without board members; their presence cannot be negotiated. For the chair, the meeting is the forum for guiding the board into action. The chief executive is the catalyst for the meeting and helps the board to focus on key issues. Numerous outsiders have a stake in successful board meetings and it is necessary to understand who can or should be present and who is not welcome. This chapter also includes a discussion on the guidelines for meeting attendance and acceptable boardroom behavior.

Board meetings are not the only meetings where board members congregate. Each board member can find him- or herself in committee meetings or executive sessions, at retreats, and other special meetings. Chapter 6 discusses the particular demands and characteristics of these sessions where board members can be vital participants.

Boardroom Q&As present in quick outline format board meeting problems common to just about any board. Whether it is poor chair performance, how to motivate board members to attend meetings, or dealing with conflicts of interest, this short question-and-answer "session" provides an easy tool to bring into the boardroom to promote board discussion.

Also included are appendices to the text, with sample documents, a glossary of terms, and suggested resources for further study.

Meet Smarter: A Guide to Better Nonprofit Board Meetings offers practical guidelines for new nonprofits and their boards with little or no experience in running meetings. In addition, the book offers helpful suggestions to the more seasoned practitioner looking for information on specific board meeting issues or ways to step away from routine methods that are no longer efficient. The book is directed to the various participants in board meetings who have a clear, vested interest in making them work: the chief executive, the board chair, and, naturally, individual board members. Each player has a different stake in ensuring that appropriate issues receive adequate attention and that the board does not allow function to get bogged down by form. Pages viii – xi provide a helpful roadmap for readers to identify the sections of the book that are of most interest to them.

Designed for the nonprofit sector in general, *Meet Smarter* takes a simple approach to a myriad of meeting-related topics and provides helpful lists, sample documents, and discussion questions for the board to address. Its purpose is to invite board members, chairs, and chief executives to analyze their meetings and whether or not these meetings can be improved. For boards with meeting problems, it is important to recognize them, accept their presence, but feel free to change old traditions. Sometimes meetings turn out to be the external expressions of other challenges with which the board may be struggling; for instance, a power struggle between board members and the executive committee. Other times, poorly managed meetings turn into unnecessary stumbling blocks to achieving the board's objectives. Without a thorough understanding of the role of a meeting and without expecting actual and concrete outcomes, it can certainly be difficult to change bad meeting habits. Boards should evaluate their meetings and make a commitment to turn them into productive and enjoyable events that shape the future of the organization.

And finally, this book is dedicated to the numerous board and staff members who have contacted BoardSource since 1988, often unintentionally educating us about the challenges they struggle with in their boardrooms. Their experiences and frustrations have been the major impetus to create this resource.

IMPORTANCE AND FUNCTION OF BOARD MEETINGS

Every incorporated nonprofit is required to have a board. As there are no owners in a nonprofit organization — not counting the stakeholders and the constituencies as the symbolic owners — the board acts in the capacity of a front-runner that is legally accountable for what happens in the organization. Groups with such a responsibility must find a setting to exercise that duty. It happens at a board meeting.

A board cannot perform without a meeting. A meeting is the place for a board to make decisions; a place where individual board members consolidate into the group that is responsible and liable for the organization. A meeting is where the board performs its role as the policy maker, sets the direction for the organization, defines the ethical guidelines, oversees the activities, and feeds into its own well-being. Together, the group acts as the board. Individually, members cannot make organizational decisions on behalf of the board. Individual board members, however, can perform certain tasks on behalf of the board outside of the meeting room, such as fundraising, advocacy, or programmatic volunteer efforts.

Meeting attendance is not optional. It is an obligation expected of every board member. Individual board members are bound by their duty of care, a legal obligation that defines the attention, thought, and consideration that they must exercise in their role as the guardians of the organization. In practice this means that a board member comes prepared to meetings, asks probing questions, pays attention, and makes decisions according to his or her best judgment. Coming prepared means that the member is familiar with the agenda, has read the board packet, and has completed any assignments from the previous meeting.

Generally, all of the board's activities cannot be accomplished in a meeting that lasts only a few hours. Therefore, there are individuals, task forces, and committees that carry out the decisions that already took place in the boardroom or that prepare the work for the full board to act on at the next meeting. It all culminates, hopefully, in a masterfully conducted board meeting where every minute is spent on issues that advance the mission of the organization. Too ideal? For boards not yet there, this book can help structure meetings in a manner that can bring boards closer to that ideal.

A board meeting also serves the role of gathering together the decision makers and allows them to interact in a manner that triggers productive communication and teamwork. During a board meeting, members get to know their peers and the way they operate. Developing personal contact between fellow members can lead to board work that is more down-to-earth. However, with any group dynamic, board meetings can be fraught with confrontations and tough challenges. But when there is a mutual goal, group members need to be able to work together and not let personal differences create obstacles for achieving that goal.

The board's role is to advance the mission of the nonprofit organization it governs. All decisions and actions ultimately are supposed to reflect and support that mission. When this philosophy is incorporated into the meeting, the meeting will start with the right foot forward. As a reminder, some boards print the mission statement atop the meeting agenda, meeting minutes, and on the nonprofit's letterhead. It may be printed on a poster on the wall of the boardroom. The board can also include "mission moments" in the meeting — short testimonials to demonstrate the connection between the organization and constituents in order to draw the link between the programs and their outcomes. Keeping the mission message in the minds of the decision makers ensures that the purpose of the organization is not overlooked.

In the end, a board meeting is a session where those most concerned and interested in the future of the organization get together to help shape that future. When properly orchestrated, wonderful things can happen around the board table during a few hours each year.

1.
Legal Framework of Meetings

It is natural that laws and statutes want to have a say in how boards run their meetings — at least some aspects of them. If a board meeting is the authoritative and legitimate setting for making organizational decisions by a body that is responsible for that organization, a legal framework can provide support and standardized guidance. It can also provide some comfort for those founders and new board members who are struggling with their first endeavor and have no direction on how to proceed. Understanding the purpose of the laws and their relationship to good practices is necessary for all meeting participants.

THE LEGAL AUTHORITY OVER BOARD MEETINGS

Neither federal laws nor the Internal Revenue Service addresses nonprofit board meeting structures and processes. Federal laws regulate many a strange issue but they have no interest in setting the rules for how nonprofits run their meetings. However, since most nonprofits are organized as nonprofit corporations, they are therefore subject to the laws of the state where they are incorporated. This book touches on several of the issues that state laws address — frequency of meetings, quorums, majority rule, and proxy votes, among others.

The BoardSource Knowledge Center has helped thousands of nonprofits with questions relating to legal regulations. The most important answer to these questions is not only to know the laws but to realize what their function is. Laws do not offer the *best* solution for nonprofits. Laws simply set the limits for the least acceptable manner in which to operate. Laws give only *de minimis* — or minimum — values for a case. For example, if a state law says that a nonprofit must have at least three members on its board, that should not be interpreted to say that a board with three members is an ideal board. Neither does it say that a board of four or even 15 members is better. It says that with two, one, or no board members the nonprofit is functioning against the law. Many nonprofits are constantly challenged with interpretation of the law.

RUNNING MEETINGS UNDER SUNSHINE LAWS

Most states have particular regulations that apply to organizations that receive public funding called *sunshine laws*, or open meeting laws. Their purpose is to bring "sunshine" or transparency to the processes of these nonprofits and to illuminate to the public how they carry out their business. Most specifically this refers to board meetings. Nonprofits that receive government funding or government contracts are usually affected by sunshine laws.

Sunshine laws were originally created for public bodies, specifically the government. The Sunshine Act followed the passing of the Freedom of Information Act in 1966. As taxpayers, concerned Americans wanted (and still do) to feel comfortable that the government is operating in a responsible manner using their tax dollars. The same principle applies to charities that benefit from tax breaks and use tax money to advance their missions.

Some states are quite broad in their definitions of their open meeting laws; some are very detailed and meticulous. These laws may clarify what a meeting is, which meetings must be open to the public, how to post meeting notices, where and when a meeting may be held, which rules apply to executive sessions, how meeting minutes are shared, and so forth. The laws also state what the penalties are if organizations do not comply: Fines can be high and all decisions at the meeting may be voided. The Web site of the Reporters Committee for Freedom of the Press at www.rcfp.org/tapping/index.cgi is a helpful tool, providing state-by-state guidelines on sunshine laws.

Most open meeting laws provide for a venue for handling confidential issues. Each board must have the opportunity to discuss, in private, personnel (or patient) issues and records; consult with legal counsel about potential or pending court cases, security arrangements, business negotiations, chief executive compensation, and performance discussions; and address other confidential issues. Social gatherings of board members and educational meetings, however, are not usually covered by sunshine laws.

WHAT DO THE SUNSHINE LAWS ACTUALLY SAY?

Below are some examples of the level of specificity each state may reach in its respective sunshine laws.

California law goes into minute details about an acceptable location for a board meeting. Oregon requires sign language interpreters to be present if a deaf person indicates that he or she will attend. In Utah, names of citizens who speak during the meeting must be included in the minutes. Wisconsin requires only two hours of notice before a meeting. Virginia lists over two dozen situations that qualify as reasons for closed meetings. In Colorado, if e-mail is used to discuss public business, it counts as a meeting and is therefore public. In Michigan, Veteran's Trust Fund does not have to follow the sunshine laws; in Mississippi there are specific exceptions for hospital boards.

Of course, the purpose of the sunshine laws is not to create an opportunity for disgruntled staff members or unhappy constituents to disrupt business proceedings. To keep meetings professional and civil, the board should clarify the kind of behavior allowed in the boardroom. For example, attendees may be allowed to make comments at the end of the meeting. Board members should pay special attention that they stay in line and that they run an effective and efficient meeting. If the board meeting is going to operate in a glass bowl, why not show the board's best side to those who are watching? Who knows, the media might also be in attendance.

WHAT SHOULD THE BYLAWS SAY ABOUT BOARD MEETINGS?

The best way for any organization to reconcile existing laws with its own needs is to study the laws; discuss openly what works best; discuss what options provide the most equitable, ethical, or reasonable guidelines; and then clearly define the chosen approach in the bylaws. For instance, the bylaws should state whether the board follows a particular parliamentary guide or relies on reaching decisions by other methods. Bylaws serve as the internal and binding legal document for the board and are not permitted to contradict state laws.

The bylaws must provide clear guidance for how a board goes about making decisions; for example, explaining that the board uses the consensus-building method to reach agreements. The bylaws should not, however, get into the nitty-gritty aspect of process and procedure. Those should be clarified in separate guidelines, policies, and resolutions and shared with new and present board members in a separate policy manual or the board handbook. The bylaws should cover certain issues that tend to create contentions among board members when disagreements surface. These specific areas may deal with the method of selecting board members, how to enforce term limits, or when to remove a board member. If the bylaws do not address these issues, board meetings may turn into battlegrounds or a member may question the validity of a decision afterwards.

If the bylaws do not address state law issues dealing with meetings, normally the law ends up determining the rules. The bylaws should not contradict the law but can be stricter than the law. Besides addressing parameters for how often the board meets and what the quorum and voting requirements are, the bylaws should also clarify whether the board may meet via teleconference or rely on other technological means to bring board members together. They should clarify who can call a special meeting, whether action can be taken without a meeting, and what happens to members who miss meetings. They should not specify the dates or places of meetings, how to write minutes, or set agendas ahead of time. For more information on nonprofit bylaws, see the Suggested Resources on page 79.

2.
Planning a Meeting

The scouts say it best: Be prepared. Meetings require advance preparation to ensure that they are productive, stay on course, and receive full participation from all attendees. The most effective board meetings happen after successfully coordinated efforts of board and staff. There must be someone authorized or expected to call the meeting, compile materials, set the agenda, and handle all the logistics. And participants must do their share and do their homework. Orchestration of a board meeting requires time, money, and sweat equity.

According to a BoardSource survey, a nonprofit chief executive, on average, spends well over eight hours per week on governance issues. Meeting preparation is one part of that. In many organizations, the weeks prior to board meetings contain the most hectic hours for the chief executive.

WHAT IS THE PURPOSE OF THIS MEETING?

Not all meetings that bring board members together fit the same mold. There are numerous purposes for the board to convene (and beyond that, each meeting may have multiple agenda items). The purpose then determines the extent of advance preparation and expectations for the outcomes. Some meetings may only require part of the board to be present (e.g., a committee meeting).

Particularly for boards that are hands-on with little or no staff to carry out decisions, meetings can have a variety of objectives. Some may be purely for exchange of information and preparation purposes. Certain issues — strategic planning, capital campaigns, major acquisitions — need thorough research and discussion even before a decision can be made to launch the endeavor. At this type of meeting, it is understood ahead of time that no voting will take place at the end of the meeting.

Some meetings may be called simply to share information. Information sharing in most cases is easiest to accomplish via phone, e-mail, or in writing. Many local community boards, however, find it constructive to get together when important announcements are made or new issues surface that may have major implications for the organization or the board as a whole. The benefits of an information-sharing gathering may turn out to be a demonstration of responsiveness to community concerns or simply to get buy-in or support for an initiative.

Boards that meet only quarterly usually convene for full-blown board meetings where deliberation leads to a final decision — or to a decision that necessitates further research before a final vote can be cast. For these boards, most of the information sharing and preparation takes place between board meetings.

Every board, without a doubt, can benefit from a retreat or board training. This provides the board an opportunity to get outside of the board room and reflect on its role, engage in self-assessment, discuss recruitment or fundraising challenges, explore strategic issues facing the organization, or talk about any other matters that require more time for reflection than a regular meeting can allow. For more on retreats and other meetings, see Chapter 6.

When determining the purpose of the meeting, it is necessary also to clarify the expected outcomes. The goals for a retreat would be very different from those of an informational gathering. Tying expectations to purpose helps the participants prepare in an effective manner and helps to evaluate (postmeeting) whether the goals and objectives were met.

HOW OFTEN SHOULD A BOARD MEET?

How often a board needs to meet depends on many factors. Some relate to internal issues, some to external demands. Some meeting frequencies are structural; others relate to the phase in the board's life cycle. Some are directly tied to the capacity of the board; others are determined by the load the staff can take in managing the operations. Whether the organization is local, national, or international also influences meeting frequency.

State laws, in many cases, require that nonprofits conduct only an annual meeting. While it would be hard to imagine that a conscientious board could carry out all of its duties and oversight at one yearly meeting, important decisions are often made at annual meetings — electing new board members and officers, among other things. At a minimum, every board must have its annual meeting.

The most important factor that determines how often the board should meet is the amount of work that needs to be accomplished. Different boards are involved in different activities. For instance, a founding board is likely to meet frequently — perhaps as often as once a month — during the start-up phase when the future of the organization is being planned and all the processes and policies are being drafted. This type of board may also have to manage all of the logistical matters of establishing the physical working space. In addition, with no staff to share the workload, the board may have to divide operational tasks between individuals and committees or task forces to ensure that everything gets done. For a more mature board with sufficient staff to handle all operational issues, the board may meet quarterly and only focus on bigger critical issues, such as approving financial statements and preparing the organization for the future.

A board that is going through an internal shake-up or is trying to meet an organizational challenge may need to increase the number of meetings from the regular schedule. Perhaps the board is losing a key member, the chief executive has resigned on short notice, or the board is in the middle of a strategic planning process. Flexibility and possibly an additional time commitment are necessary if the full board's involvement is required.

Special emergencies may suddenly bring the full board together. If there is no executive committee or other processes to handle unexpected events, every board member may need to make an effort to attend and determine how to get through a sudden crisis or problematic phase.

Frequency is also a function of whether board members reside outside of the region or live in other parts of the country or the world. Regional and local boards generally meet more frequently because proximity makes it easier to convene the board, while national and international boards may find it more challenging to bring members together more than a few times a year.

It is not always easy to determine what actually requires the full board's presence or when other groups (task forces, committees, etc.) can step in to eliminate the need for gathering the full board. When setting up the yearly meeting schedule, take some time to first clarify this issue. Is the board involved in activities that cannot or should not be delegated elsewhere? Committees and task forces are there to bear a big load of board preparation work. The purpose of these subgroups is to allow the board to deal with big issues at the decision level and not have to spend valuable meeting time to dig up facts, formulate arguments, and draft final documents. Remember also that most committee members are board members, and committee meetings and board meetings together may add up to a substantial number of meetings. Active board members face burnout if their life is filled with meetings. Respect people's private lives and call a meeting only when it is necessary.

If the board meets monthly on a regular basis, it must be able to justify that frequency. If there is no staff, the board probably needs to be touching base in order to determine the next set of tasks and monitor progress. Boards that have competent staff support and an adequate and capable committee system may be able to justify meeting less frequently.

The following list (feel free to add to it) may indicate that the board meets too often. In order to determine whether the board should meet less frequently, consider these questions:

- Does the board delegate insufficiently?
- Is the board too operational?
- Does the work of the board burn out its members?
- Does the board structure its meetings poorly?
- Does the board focus on short-term issues and lose the big picture?
- Does the board add unnecessary expenses?
- Is the staff burdened with meeting preparation?
- Does the board use other venues and communication inadequately?

Some boards may not meet often enough. It is hardly adequate for most boards to meet only once a year at the legally required annual meeting. It is highly unlikely that an accountable board is able to manage its governance responsibilities along with other duties on the side in just a few hours. Under those circumstances the board may miss important yet subtle signals that something may not be right, or it can miss opportunities knocking at the door because of the board's inattention. It is also very difficult to create a sense of camaraderie among board members if the board meets so infrequently.

THE WHEN, WHERE, AND HOW OF PLANNING A MEETING

How often has a meeting been memorable because lunch was the best (or the worst) part? Perhaps the room was overwhelmingly stuffy or too cold, or the timing was complicated by work or family schedules. It is only human to be affected by the

15 Steps to a Better Meeting

The difference between an enjoyable, productive, and well-run meeting and one that finds its members nodding off is in the planning. If a board has ensured that meetings are well planned and have proper follow-up after the meeting, then the focus should be on what actually happens *in* the boardroom. Engage the board in a discussion of what would constitute a good board meeting. If the true problem is monotony, here are some suggestions to help pep up the general tone of meetings.

1. Make sure the meeting room is welcoming, seats are comfortable, and temperature is pleasant. The general atmosphere must already capture a member's interest.

2. Start on time; end on time. Respect everybody's schedules.

3. Don't meet late in the evening or early in the morning if members have difficulties staying awake. Find a compromise.

4. Use ice-breakers to set the tone for the meeting. Keep them appropriate in order not to turn off the serious-minded peers.

5. Eliminate report reading. Use a consent agenda and expect everyone to be familiar with its content.

6. If the chair is not a good meeting facilitator, tactfully suggest that someone else take the lead or rotate the job.

7. Use charts, pictures, or any other tools to capture the interest of the listeners and to keep the focus alive. Don't allow listeners to read reports during the presentation.

8. Elect a devil's advocate for the board to offer unconventional arguments, question the norm, and to bring some drama to the discussion.

9. Include in every agenda a short discussion on some controversial or passionate issue to which the board must pay attention.

10. Require that the majority of the meeting time be spent on major issues geared toward the future and not on what has already happened.

11. Invite engaging guests and speakers to liven up the discussion.

12. Good meetings have good food. Make it a rule to serve something different each time.

13. When appropriate, have "theme" meetings to cover a main issue in depth. For example, fundraising campaigns, lobbying efforts, or new marketing approaches.

14. Ensure that breaks allow members to stretch out. Have plenty of water and some snacks available.

15. Use minievaluations after every meeting. Assign the task to someone to ensure that valuable comments are shared, heard, and implemented. Periodically, conduct more thorough meeting evaluations.

If boring meetings persist, the board will gradually lose its members. If the board is missing the opportunity to vigorously engage board members at the meeting, bring the issue out in the open and make sure an item in the next agenda reads: How can the meetings be more engaging and interesting?

"peripheries" of meeting logistics, but if the organizers do not understand some basic aspects of human nature, a meeting can lose its impact. Handling board meeting logistics is usually the job of the staff. Experience can be a powerful educator and the chief executive can serve as the guide on what works and what doesn't for the board.

Numerous logistical aspects can impact a board meeting and its outcome. The main objective should be to motivate every single board member to attend the meeting, come well prepared, participate constructively, feel invigorated and energized about the work, and remember the meeting positively because of what was accomplished and because it was a pleasant and conducive place to work at that moment. Professional attitude and experienced meeting management can help make this a reality.

TIMING: WHEN SHOULD THE MEETING HAPPEN?

The optimal time to get every board member to come to a meeting can be a major challenge and only by planning can the board make it happen. The schedule may need to accommodate busy business people who travel often, employees who may have difficulties with leaving their work during business hours, parents who cannot leave children alone at night, young members who are still in class during afternoon hours, members who rely on public transportation schedules, and so on.

The board should determine the schedule *together* and get feedback from everyone. Some members may prefer to meet midday; others may be able to come only in the evening; some may choose weekends. Individual members may need to demonstrate a little flexibility — particularly those who have to travel long distances. But make an attempt to meet them half way. The board may want to change the timing for some meetings in order to accomodate those participants who are always making a compromise. If a board has an established meeting schedule, prospective members should be told before they accept the nomination.

When looking at the annual calendar, take into account major vacation periods and special religious holidays. Some grass-roots boards have policies that compensate financially challenged members for lost working hours or facilitate babysitting accommodations.

HOW LONG SHOULD THE MEETING LAST?

The agenda is the key tool that determines the length of the meeting. Naturally, the goal is to maximize the use of time. There needs to be a balance between getting business done and allowing sufficient time for personal interaction. Here are some questions that could help the board determine the appropriate length for meetings.

How Often Does the Board Meet?

If it is monthly, under normal circumstances business could take an hour or so. If it is only a few times a year, the meeting could last a full day or more.

- What is the purpose of the meeting? Regularly scheduled board meetings may follow a regular pattern, but the length for special or emergency sessions is defined by the urgency and importance of the issue. Retreats can stretch out over a weekend.

- How skilled is the board chair in conducting a meeting? Keeping the discussion focused and following the agenda are some of the qualities of an able chair.

- Is the agenda appropriate? Does the board deal with board issues? Is a consent agenda used to consolidate items, leaving more time for important and timely issues?

- Is staff getting appropriate materials to board members well before the meeting? Do board members arrive well prepared? When board members familiarize themselves with the agenda items and support materials ahead of time, meeting length can be shortened.

The board chair has the major responsibility of getting everyone appropriately engaged. Without apt participation, it can be difficult to control the length of the meeting. The meeting can turn out to be a monologue presented by the chair or some other participant (lack of member engagement), a lengthy session with endless comments (lack of control), or there can be a balanced process where sharing of ideas leads to productive conclusions.

By expecting that most of the legwork of the board will take place in committees and task forces, the board is then able to focus on what it should do best: analyze recommendations, weigh the final options, and determine the directives for critical issues.

PLACE: WHERE SHOULD THE BOARD MEET?

For a national or an international organization, the location of the board meeting can have major financial implications — both for individual members and for the organization itself. If board members travel by plane or drive for hours, it may be difficult to justify going a long distance for just a two-hour meeting. If time and location dictate, some members might like to tie in other business or pleasure travel with the board meeting schedule. Arranging a meeting in a major city or vacation resort can become an added incentive to attending. If meetings are always in the same location, some board members may have a bigger burden to bear — money, time, and effort — while local members are always in a more advantaged position. If meetings take place elsewhere than where the office is, factor in the operational costs for travel and hotels for senior staff in attendance along with the expense of a suitable meeting place.

For a local organization, choosing the place to hold a meeting is a key issue. Should it happen at the office? Are there suitable conference facilities near by? If the organization's office has a large enough conference or meeting room, that can be an excellent solution. Holding meetings in the office can provide the opportunity for staff to meet the board members. Making board members more visible to staff brings the board more down to earth — even if board work mostly happens behind a closed door. Arranging for the staff to join the board for lunch or dinner provides an opportunity for board-staff interaction.

If the office cannot accommodate a full board meeting, research other options in the area. Most areas have conference facilities suitable for small and large groups and for every budget. A board member may even be able to offer his or her business site for a meeting, free of charge. Small grass-roots boards may choose to meet at the home of a board member when the cost of renting a meeting space cannot be justified — even if this is not the ideal option. Smaller boards often embrace camaraderie and cooperation, but in order to keep the business aspect of the meetings from being overcome by the social aspect, it is important that the meeting space be able to provide a congenial but private setting for serious discussion.

As with timing, it is also possible to impact attendance by changing the location every so often. If the board members live within driving distance, choose a different town for different meetings. Let board members host the meetings or let them provide valuable feedback on possible locations within their community. If the meeting location changes on a regular basis, make sure that the board has plenty of advance notice about the new location along with clear driving directions.

ADOPTING A TRAVEL REIMBURSEMENT POLICY

Board service should not create undue financial burden for any board member. Who pays for board members to travel to meetings? For large national or international boards, the issue can be significant. Before adopting a board member reimbursement policy, the board needs to look at the issue from all angles. Individual board members and the organization's budget are directly affected by this policy.

There are several options to consider when developing a reimbursement policy. The most common policy is to not reimburse expenses. According to a BoardSource survey, only 14 percent of the respondents' organizations regularly reimbursed board members for their expenses, and another 14 percent did so only if board members specifically requested it.

If a board does decide to reimburse some expenses, it should explain the details in a separate policy. What expenses should be reimbursed? The policy may stipulate a ceiling per board member per meeting, determine a manageable per diem, or clarify the fine points of what is acceptable and what is not. These points may cover mileage reimbursement rates, a list of acceptable hotels or dollar limits for hotel stays, or whether board members are expected to fly coach. The policy may also determine a differentiation between travel to committee meetings and board meetings. Some local boards with members in the lowest income bracket have gone as far as reimbursing lost wages for the time spent in a board meeting or contributing to a babysitter fee for single parents of small children. Paying spouses' expenses should be justified judiciously. If ever this were to occur, the reimbursement may turn into a compensation issue that must be reported in the Form 990.

It may seem unreasonable to expect that, without limitations, a nonprofit would generously pay all the bills of every member on a 20-member board for quarterly meetings every year. Those expenses add up very quickly and it comes out of the organization's budget. Remember: No matter how effective the board is, funders would much rather put their money behind an organization's programmatic needs.

Some boards may ask their members to pay their own expenses as a way to help cover meeting costs. This certainly is an opposite approach to compensating board members for their effort. If these expenses are a true burden, there is nothing wrong with bringing up the issue in the boardroom and turning these expenses into contributions to count as tax-deductible gifts or considering some other cost-sharing options.

If a board decides not to adopt a reimbursement policy, this must be communicated to prospective board members. Board member candidates must feel comfortable about personally assuming the future expenses associated with board meeting attendance.

HOW SHOULD THE ROOM BE SET UP?

Whether the issue is who sits where or the temperature of the room, the details can determine the attentiveness of board members during a meeting. When hierarchy matters or when it only plays a subtle role, having predetermined seating arrangements may be important. Where does the chief executive sit? Under most circumstances, the chief executive sits next to the board chair. That sends a signal that the position in the organization is crucial — even if he or she is not a voting member of the board. This seating arrangement indicates that there is an established partnership between the chair and the chief executive and it helps facilitate communication between the two. This arrangement does not necessarily apply during retreats or at some committee meetings where the board chair and the chief executive are also present.

The board may choose to have assigned seating arrangements for all participants. If so, change the order regularly. This will force different members to communicate directly with a peer who may not always share their opinions. These configurations can change the dynamics of communication channels. If seats are not assigned, simply invite board members to sit next to someone with whom they do not usually interact much or whom they do not know very well. Developing personal connections is the glue that keeps team members attached.

The traditional rule says that staff members attending, but not presenting at board meetings, should sit in the periphery and not mix with board members. A staff member or guests invited to make a presentation or participate in an important discussion should be treated with due respect. Welcome staff to sit around the same table that welcomes board members. Seat guest speakers next to the board chair. In many cases the guests will likely stay for only a portion of the meeting, but it is essential for them to understand that their role is important and appreciated during the time they are present.

Different table formations may affect the ease with which members communicate with each other. There may not be a choice in the shape of the table, but an oval, round, square, or open horseshoe shape tends to be most accommodating. The objective is to allow board members to face one another. Even for larger boards, a classroom-style seating arrangement is counterproductive. Avoid an arrangement where board members end up talking to the back of a peer and never gain eye contact with a fellow member. Seating arrangements can often influence the outcomes of meetings. If the intent of the meeting is to deliberate a sensitive issue, members should most definitely be facing one another in order to allow open discussion and eye contact.

BOARDROOM CAUSE AND EFFECT

A quick glance into the room where a board meets can tell a story.

If the board considers hierarchy important

- the board chair sits alone at the end of the table with a gavel; staff sits along the wall.

If informality drives the meeting

- the meeting is set around a working lunch or dinner meeting and board members are wearing casual clothing.

If boredom has set in

- the room is full of blank stares, slouched postures, and members taking private notes or doodling.

If the chair is not able to control the proceedings

- everyone is speaking at the same time and members demonstrate agitated body language.

If board members fidget and seem irritated

- the room is too cold, too dark, too stuffy, or the chairs are not comfortable.

Take these clues to heart and remember them when organizing the next meeting.

Physical comfort is another aspect that affects the participants. Before the meeting, test the temperature of the meeting room. Find out how to change it if it gets too hot or too cold. Remember that dim lights make people sleepy. There may not be much choice about the chairs on which attendees will sit, but test them anyway. If the organization is in the process of equipping its office conference room, do not make the mistake of choosing chairs simply for their low cost or elegance. Board members will be sitting on those chairs in that room for hours at a time, so make sure that this side of meeting planning — overall comfort — makes attending meetings a less taxing experience.

FEEDING THE BOARD

Food represents a social aspect of a board meeting. If lunch is served in the middle of a meeting, a moment is reserved when business is secondary and more relaxed conversation is on the front burner. Mealtime can be a time to build relationships and trust among board members. It is easier to relate to peers when they are able to let their guard down, exchange personal news, and talk without the constant guidance or reference from the board chair.

Within reasonable limits, it is a good idea to provide some refreshments during a meeting. Serving lunch is a given if a meeting goes through noontime. Some boards meet over dinner after working hours. If this is the case, it is important to *separate business from eating*. It can be difficult to get the board's full attention on business if the participants are worrying about their salad dressing. Provide light breakfast items if the meeting starts early in the morning and serve coffee, water, and soft drinks during breaks. If wine is offered at the meeting, wait to serve it until the end of the business — and always provide a soft drink alternative. These little measures help keep boredom and fatigue outside of the meeting room.

HOW MUCH WILL IT COST?

Board meetings cost money — there is no way around it. Make sure that the annual governance budget includes a "meetings" item. Keep track of the current or previous year's receipts and it will be easier to budget expenses for the following year.

Larger boards naturally mean larger expenses. The items to factor into the budget are the cost of a meeting room, catering, photocopying, and postage for mailing out board packets if they are not sent electronically. Costs for teleconferencing and videoconferencing also must be accounted for. If the board does in fact have a travel reimbursement policy, as discussed earlier in the book, all compensation expenses should be included as a line item in the meetings budget. Staff may spend a significant amount of time preparing for the meetings so staff time should be anticipated and accounted for.

The budget may also need to include any additional operating costs for committee meetings. Because the cost of meetings comes from the organizational budget, carefully calculate where the line is between appropriate and adequate. Some board members may be used to expensive restaurants and fancy accommodations in their private lives or business connections. This does not mean that the board needs to follow the example and cater to the members' personal preferences. Each organization must determine for itself what standards it considers appropriate. For instance, the board of a community soup kitchen would not bring in the town's famed caterer to feed its board members. At the same time, a symphony orchestra's board would probably not snack on hot dogs during its meeting.

HOLDING ELECTRONIC BOARD MEETINGS

Sometimes it is impossible for a board member to be physically present at a board meeting, whether due to geography, an unavoidable business conflict, or personal matters. Are there any other legally acceptable ways to convene a meeting without every member being physically present?

First, check what the state's laws say. Some state statutes recognize the legitimacy of teleconference or videoconference attendance. As long as it is possible to establish a quorum, allow everyone to express opinions separately, keep track of the flow of the meeting and voting results, and produce accurate minutes afterwards, these formats allow everyone to hear each other and a board member to participate from a distant location.

Teleconferencing and videoconferencing have their place, but they should not replace the traditional face-to-face meetings on a regular basis. They can bring the board together quickly in an emergency and save costs for meetings by cutting down long-distance travel. They are helpful for keeping committees and task forces in touch in between regular meetings. It is not always necessary for everyone to sit in the same room to get business done. Especially after September 11, many boards have considered these options to alleviate fears of traveling and the high costs involved.

The following are some suggestions to incorporate into the board's next teleconference or videoconference.

Tips for teleconferencing

- Be mindful of different time zones. Choose a convenient hour for everyone to be a part of the meeting.

- The chair should pay special attention to how to involve all board members.

- Take a roll call to establish a quorum.

- Ask every speaker to first identify him- or herself before making a comment.

- Don't allow people to speak at the same time.

- Ask members to call from a quiet location and speak clearly.

- Don't use teleconferencing for major planning meetings or for sorting out a conflict.

- Follow up with minutes if decisions were made.

Tips for videoconferencing

- Have a contingency plan in case contact is lost or interrupted.

- Practice and test the system and tech sites ahead of time.

- Try to find convenient contact sites for members, or organize regional contact points.

- Include expenses in the budget.

- Don't use videoconferencing for large boards.

Board meeting logistics should not end up turning board members away or inhibit their productivity and creativity. There is an expectation that board members place

E-MAIL OR ELECTRONIC MEETING CHALLENGES

Without a doubt, e-mail meetings will be more legally acceptable in the future as technology continues to advance. Here are some questions that need to be answered.

- How long should meetings last? Are they synchronistic (everyone communicating simultaneously in different places) or nonsynchronistic (everyone communicating at different times at different places)?

- Are there board members who do not have computer access or are not particularly comfortable with computers? How should they be accommodated?

- Is the meeting ready to start as soon as a quorum is sufficient?

- Should e-mails be addressed only to the chair? Is it the chair's job to then distribute the e-mails to board members in a chronological order?

- How can the chair deal with unwieldy comments that veer off the topic, are too long, or unintelligible?

- What is the best process to authenticate the identity of a voter?

- How should the chair determine that the meeting is over in order not to cut off any valuable comments?

- How can the board meetings remain fun?

- Should there be a new format for the minutes? Is there a willing individual to undertake the job of compiling the minutes?

- Are there certain agenda items that new board members may be better served discussing face to face?

Needless to say, it is imperative to clarify the standards and practices of e-meetings in the bylaws (as long as the state laws allow them) and create a clear procedure document outlining all the details. As new issues surface, remember to revise the procedure document.

the needs of the organization on top of their own priorities, and therefore express understanding and flexibility if all of their comfort zone issues are not included in the meeting arrangements. At the same time, there is no need to expect that individual board members suffer personally from their board service. Logistical issues — whether food preferences, sensitivity to air conditioning, or financial matters — should facilitate a productive working environment. It is perfectly acceptable to expect board members to see themselves as servants of the organization, not as its major beneficiaries.

3.
Meeting Documentation and Board Communications

Communication between board members happens on a continuum, and information exchange is a constant activity during and in between meetings. The goal is to make communication as efficient as possible. This can be achieved by preparing documents that are accurate and comprehensible. The documents provide a permanent record of the board's activities, discussions, and decisions and, if properly kept, can provide the board with some legal protection. In addition to the standard board documents (meeting agendas, board minutes, board packets, and meeting reports), this chapter discusses the benefits of using consent agendas and using electronic communication for exchange in between board meetings.

CREATING MEETING AGENDAS

Despite the purpose of the meeting, there needs to be an agenda. The agenda is the road map — the reminder for the chair to keep the meeting moving forward and the guide for the participants to know what to expect next. Reviewing the agenda prior to a meeting helps board members prepare mentally for upcoming discussions.

To maximize participation of all members of the board in all meetings, set the meeting schedule at least a year ahead of time. This may sound daunting, but first consider that certain issues come up every spring or fall (such as approving the annual budget or board elections) so some agenda items can be determined far in advance by necessity.

Who should draft the agenda? In most organizations the chair and the chief executive share the effort. In a discussion between the two, the chair ensures that topics included are appropriate for the board and that all relevant issues are incorporated. The chief executive adds topics that the board would not otherwise know, such as the organization's operational challenges and successes since the last meeting, and possible future issues the board should be prepared to tackle. Together the two leaders can prioritize the issues while ensuring that the agenda is not too staff-driven or operational but still includes the chief executive's internal perspective.

A board meeting agenda must convey the basic logistics for the coming meeting: where and when the meeting takes place. The agenda should clarify the type of meeting it is (board meeting, board retreat, etc.) and identify the general business: the call to order, approval of last minutes, and the adjournment. An agenda should also list the main items needing attention. As a helpful guide, it may indicate the time allotted for each item and whether the item is there for discussion, information, or action. Consider including the most important business at the beginning of the agenda to ensure that the board does not run out of time at the end or miss those board members who may need to leave meetings early in order to catch a plane or relieve a babysitter. See page 67 for sample meeting agendas.

A board meeting agenda must be focused on the future. It should not dwell on the past and rehash what has already happened. A cardinal mistake in drafting agendas is to dedicate 80 percent of the meeting time to committee reports. The board is responsible for paving the future for the organization and it can only do so if it focuses on issues that are either waiting to happen or that it wants to happen. These issues affect the sustainability of the organization and should be anticipated by the board in a purposeful manner.

Board members may sometimes request that an item be added to the agenda. It is the board chair who reviews those requests and determines whether they require discussion by the full board or whether the issue can be handled directly with the board member or referred to a committee. It is possible also that a constituent, client, or a customer may want the board to address an issue at the next meeting. Once again, the chair is in the best position to respond. He or she may determine that the request is a management matter and refer the individual to the chief executive. If the issue potentially has an organizationwide impact, it may be appropriate for the full board to be briefed about it and determine a course of action.

The strategic plan or framework is a key reference that should be reflected in the agenda. An organization should not go through the time and trouble of a strategic planning process and then ignore the results. Thorough planning has already identified the key topics that the board must include on its radar screen. The agenda should fit into the overall scheme that the board must follow. The board should be on top of the relevant issues and should not spend valuable meeting time discussing trivial matters that are better handled via e-mail, phone calls, or committee deliberations.

Strategically thinking boards are constantly ahead of the game and their meeting agendas will reflect this attitude. While still giving proper attention to the board's oversight responsibilities, these boards save a major part of the meeting for issue discussions that are timely and geared toward the next phase where the organization wants to be. If the organization is in the middle of a controversy or a struggle, the board looks at options for getting it back on track to meet the next challenges that are still in the pipeline.

CONSENT AGENDAS: WHAT ARE THEY FOR?

Many boards have realized that time is a scarce commodity and to benefit fully from their busy board members, they must use every minute of the meeting strategically and purposefully. This is where the consent agenda can help.

A consent agenda appears as one section or one subject in the meeting agenda. Usually it is placed at the very beginning of the agenda to let the board subsequently continue on with other issues that need special attention.

Consent agendas allow the board to group standard, regular, and routine items under one heading and pass that "package" with one vote. The important feature of these items is that none of them should require any discussion. When the chair brings the consent agenda to a vote, if one board member has a question concerning an item included in the consent agenda, that item gets pulled out and handled separately. This last issue can be a challenge for boards that are not comfortable and totally familiar with the process. But with practice, education, and patience, a board will soon learn to appreciate this feature and the impact it has on the way meetings are run.

A standard consent agenda could include

- committee and chief executive reports,

- approval of the minutes from the last meeting,

- any routine documents that simply need to get recorded in the minutes, and

- other items that have previously gone through thorough deliberation and simply need the final seal of approval by the board.

The board needs to be familiar and comfortable with each item it votes on in the consent agenda. This level of familiarity is possible to achieve when the documents and reports have been distributed to every board member well in advance of the meeting as part of the overall board packet. The time for the board to ask questions about items on the consent agenda is in the days and weeks before the meeting. By using e-mail or a phone call to clarify a point or suggest a correction in the minutes, the person responsible for the agenda should then make the necessary changes and share the corrected version with all board members before the meeting. The board meeting is not the ideal place to handle these operational issues.

By using consent agendas, a board can save critical time for discussion of issues that need attention. Removing committee reports from the main agenda may first make committee chairs feel as if their work is not appreciated. Including the report in the consent agenda does not mean a committee's work on a crucial issue should be ignored and tabled. On the contrary, a committee's recommendation or analysis may be the focal point of the board's next discussion. Once the committee's report has been recorded, the board can move forward on the issue. At the same time, it is not uncommon for the next meeting to come and go without something extremely serious or important being included in a committee report. It makes sense to read that report in a more comfortable setting prior to a short board meeting rather than have it take up precious meeting time.

Another advantage to the consent agenda is the elimination of inactive participation. Meetings can become boring when members are required to sit still and listen to reports. Committee reports rarely make the boardroom burst into laughter because of their special humor or captivating case studies. Board members need to be stimulated and that stimulation comes from participation in an engaging debate or discussion.

PREPARING BOARD PACKETS

To ensure board members come to a meeting well prepared and ready to participate, board packets should be mailed out to members well in advance. The board packet is the main tool to prepare members of the board for fruitful discussion. Information included in the packet should contain all of the necessary materials and documents that address issues listed in the agenda, with the agenda itself being the main document included.

Besides the agenda, the packet should include copies of committee reports; the operational report from the chief executive; minutes from the last meeting; any support and background information on the main business items; and other helpful data, articles, and newsletters that advance board members' familiarity with the purpose of the meeting.

In most organizations the staff is responsible, as well as best equipped, to compile the packets. The chief executive is the key person to keep the board informed of relevant issues. He or she has already developed the agenda with the chair and is tuned to the details of the next meeting. The staff has the resources and the files that feed into board education and information. They are involved in industry issues that the board needs to understand along with other matters that closely relate to the organization. The staff serves as the support mechanism for board operations and ensures that every board member has what is needed to come prepared to the meeting. It is the job of the chair and the chief executive to review the board packet information and ensure that the board isn't bogged down with administrative information, but that board members are focused on their governance and oversight responsibilities.

Electronic transmittal of board packets has become a popular mode of distribution. This distribution channel can help to save time, postage, and, theoretically, the need for multiple hard copies. Experience has shown, however, that board members will likely still want to print out the e-mails to fill their paper files and may need to have the materials available at the meeting.

KEEPING BOARD MEETING MINUTES

WHY KEEP MINUTES?

Minutes form a permanent record of a board meeting. They provide practical information about when the meeting took place, who was present, and what actually happened in the boardroom. They serve as the memory of the meeting. Minutes are a legal document approved by the board and **can be used as support documents in the courtroom** — the single most powerful message of the legal authority of minutes.

WHAT SHOULD BE INCLUDED IN THE MINUTES?

While content can vary based on each individual organization, the basic elements of good minutes include

- name of the organization

- date and time of meeting

- board members in attendance, excused, and absent

- existence of a quorum

- action steps: motions made and by whom; brief account of any debate; voting results; names of abstainers and dissenters

- reports and documents introduced

- future action steps

- time meeting ended

- signature of secretary and chair

Imagine a situation where meeting minutes are not kept. Sometime afterwards, one of the board members questions the direction another member is taking while implementing a decision. Both board members have a different but firm view of what was decided. Because there was no record, they cannot reconcile and verify the facts. In another case, a board member wants to prove to his lawyer that he has been active against an initiative during several meetings, but because no minutes exist, he is not able to do so. In other situations, it may become necessary to substantiate the timing when a policy was amended and approved. If minutes were not kept, this information would not be obtainable because lack of records won't allow it.

The above examples are just a few of the possible situations where clear meeting minutes could have saved the face of a board member, eliminated unnecessary confusion and time loss, and comforted (or brought a cold sweat to the brow of) a board member who was implicated in a lawsuit. Minutes are one of the potentially best protective mechanisms for board members. If a board keeps haphazard minutes, this document does not help much when help is needed. As long as a board includes all the needed ingredients in the document — plus avoids unnecessary and onerous comments — and if every board member reads the minutes before approving them, there is potential for a solid way not only to keep track of board decisions but to indicate which board member approved an action, was against an action, or was absent from the meeting. Verification of the meeting minutes and their thoroughness should be a concern for every board member before anyone needs to rely on them for help in the future.

IS THERE A "BEST" WAY TO TAKE AND KEEP MINUTES?

Two things are necessary for good and accurate record keeping: 1) a competent person to take the minutes, and 2) a format that delivers readable and understandable information. Traditionally, the secretary of the board keeps the minutes. Today, more often a staff member may handle this task. This person could be the executive assistant or a designated board liaison allowing the board secretary and the chief executive to participate fully in the meeting without having to focus on recording the session.

If a board handles confidential issues, it should call an executive session. Any confidential notes or documents as a result would not be attached to the board meeting minutes and therefore — depending on the case — would remain protected under open meeting laws and during a possible court hearing.

After the contents of the minutes have been clarified (see the previous page for a list of items), it is easier to decide on the format. A suitable format reflects the culture of the board and presents the facts in a concise and easily referenced manner. While deciding on a format, keep in mind that this document — despite its name — is not a story of every minute that was spent in the meeting; it is not a verbatim account. Members should not have to plow through pages and pages of who said what to whom and when. The minutes focus on decisions made and actions taken. Direct quotes during debate are not usually desirable, as they could hinder honest and candid dialogue. Summaries of discussions should be objectively reported.

To remain organized and to allow the minutes to serve as reference documents, the secretary should ensure that all minutes are kept in a "minutes book." This book may be a binder that contains the record of all minutes or an electronic file made accessible to all board members via an intranet, a board-only Web site, or on demand. If the minutes refer to the budget under discussion, the book or the file should contain the budget document as an attachment. The same is true for all other documents referenced in the minutes. The minutes book is a chronological record of all decisions and new or amended policies, when board members or officers were elected, and who was present at each meeting and how he or she voted on a specific issue. With an adequate recording of these facts, the board can remain confident that its board history is always within reach. The compilation should be available for legal review and can be used as a tool for board orientation. Minutes can also help absent board members stay on track and remain familiar with board decisions.

A board member's performance is also recorded in the minutes. If a board member is shy about asking questions when he or she does not understand a point and votes "with the flow," that uninformed vote gets recorded. An understanding that the minutes are a record of what happened should force individual board members to pay attention to the influence and strength of the document. Bashfulness is not an excuse in the boardroom: If a member doesn't understand something, he or she should ask a question and vote only when there is a comfort level with the decision. It is important then to make sure the vote is recorded in the minutes.

All minutes ultimately must be approved by the board. As has been previously emphasized, do not carry a discussion of the details of the minutes during the meeting. Circulation and review of the minutes should happen between meetings. A person should be tasked with getting a copy of the draft to each board member and the chief executive for checkup and possible comments. In order to avoid numerous back-and-forths, a simple format and agreement on how much detail is to be included is necessary.

E-mailing board minutes to board members is the simplest and quickest way to get feedback and to redistribute the document when changes are recommended. The final version is then included in the consent agenda and should not cause any additional discussion in the boardroom. If it seems that getting minutes approved becomes too laborious a job, it may be necessary to put the issue on the main agenda and have the full board decide on a mutually acceptable solution for the process and overall contents for the minutes.

If a board is subject to sunshine laws, it most likely is required to publicly post its minutes. Each board should know what its state laws require. Some boards consider it a necessary sign of transparency to share board meeting minutes with all constituents and post meeting minutes on their Web site. Keep in mind, however, that confidential issues belong in an executive session. Sharing the minutes is one way to ensure that they are accurate, informative, and reflect properly on your board's priorities.

TAPE RECORDING MEETINGS

Boards using tape recorders in the meeting room should make sure that all board members are aware of the taping and that the pros and cons of this practice have been thoroughly weighed. Boards that deal with mounds of detailed information (e.g., foundation boards evaluating grant proposals or meetings where complicated financial transactions are discussed) may find it helpful to record the minutiae to facilitate the work of developing accurate minutes. The tape should not serve as the final record because it is not easily and quickly referenced. On the other hand, a tape recorder may hinder open discussion and tame otherwise lively members from expressing their opinions in fear of comments taken out of context or threat of personal liability. If a board uses tapes, a policy of how to deal with the tapes afterwards should be adopted. When are they destroyed and who may do it? A policy eliminates the risk of tapes being destroyed prematurely or by an unauthorized person who is intending to expunge possible evidence.

GENERATING BOARD REPORTS

Many standard board meeting agendas are inundated with reports: committee reports, the treasurer's report, and the chief executive's report. Clearly, reports have a role in meetings, but if they dominate a meeting, they keep the board looking at the past. As was previously suggested, **standard board-related reports should be included in the consent agenda.** The following section discusses the format and the purpose of these reports.

The main work of the board often happens in committees and task forces. These work groups are essential for getting the board's chores accomplished. The board delegates certain tasks or activities to these groups and usually expects to hear the results or progress at a future time. Without a common agreement on what the objective of these reports should be and how to best present the relevant data, reports may become filled with pages of unnecessary details and may be presented in numerous formats that make it difficult to keep track of project advancement.

The purpose of a committee report is to keep the board informed on the evolution of a project, to communicate the results of a specific task that the committee undertook, to engage the board in discussion of an issue, or to present recommendations for board action. If nothing has happened since the last meeting, no report should be necessary.

The report is not the same as committee meeting minutes. The minutes are the record of what happened during the meeting. Some committee meetings do not need official minutes, but they simply keep notes for future reference and as an indication that the group has been in contact. The board does not need to know those details, but requires a consolidated message (i.e., the report) that the group wants to confer to the rest of the board.

It makes sense to develop a format for all committee reports or at least set clear guidelines on what is relevant and essential. Using a standard software program (the board should decide on a Windows-, or Mac-based software) or creating a template for committee members to fill in can alleviate some of the work for the group's chair. Usually the committee or task-force chair is responsible for creating the report, preparing the meeting agenda, and ensuring that the committee's charge gets carried out.

COMMUNICATING ELECTRONICALLY BETWEEN MEETINGS

For most boards, it is imperative that activity continues between meetings and information and documents are shared. Minutes need to be circulated before the next session. Meeting planners need feedback on logistical issues. The chair needs to follow up on board assignments. Some matters need not enter the boardroom and should only be handled outside of official sessions.

Without a doubt, today the electronic medium is the most efficient, cost-effective, and rapid way to communicate in between meetings. Of course there are still boards and board members who are not computer savvy or do not have the needed equipment. Fortunately, these cases are more and more often becoming the exception. Staff can be helpful in guiding board members to locations where they can access a computer. This can include the organization's own offices, local affiliates, and public libraries. If there are some board members who simply are not able to take advantage of these facilities, the traditional methods of mailing or faxing materials and communicating via phone are tried and true solutions.

Creating a special section on the organization's Web site, accessible only to board members, or establishing an intranet specifically for the board provides a secure and easy location for governance materials. A listserv or a chat room can be part of that structure and allows board members to communicate with each other in real time or over the course of time while keeping a permanent record. Electronic communication also helps overcome time zone differences.

Simple e-mails provide another method of communication. Documents can be shared and board members can suggest future agenda items. This is also a forum for members to share personal news with colleagues. To avoid creating small group discussions on an issue that excludes other board members, it must be understood and agreed upon that messages are to be shared with everyone. It's as simple as using a group address and clicking on the "Reply All" button when sending or responding to an e-mail. Because of the ease and rapid exchanges possible with e-mail and all Web-based communication, one can hope that communication between board meetings will become less of a burden, time constraint, or hazard for excluding others.

4.
Meeting Structure, Decision Making, and Voting

A board has total freedom to choose its method for conducting its meetings, as long as all legal requirements and ethical expectations are met. Whether a board chooses to follow a strict parliamentary procedure or take a more relaxed approach, structure and order in the boardroom keep proceedings from getting out of hand and help in guiding the decision-making process. This chapter discusses the use of parliamentary procedure and explores a variety of decision-making and voting practices. It also looks at how a board's culture and structure affect the way that work is accomplished.

BUSINESS VS. SOCIAL: CREATING A FINE BALANCE

How well board members carry out their duties, communicate with each other, work as a team, or solve problems are all closely related to the board's culture. These factors can either result in an efficient and productive team that works well together or a dysfunctional and unproductive group. By looking at a board's processes in more detail, it is possible to determine whether it is a group hung up on procedures, functioning more as a private social club, or one that is continuously accomplishing something important.

Running a meeting like a neighborhood social gathering, however, is not the objective — no matter how enjoyable it can be. The board should meet for business reasons. Every board meeting should include some serious and often complicated matters that require the full attention of every member. If the environment is not conducive to business, haphazard decisions can result. If the culture of the board is too relaxed, it may be easy to step out of line and forget or ignore the legal aspects required for a board meeting.

For some boards it may be helpful to set a dress code for board meetings. This can be communicated at a board member orientation or as part of casual conversation to new recruits. Whether it's business attire or more casual clothing, having everyone "fit in" eliminates any unnecessary judgment of a peer's importance or role on the board.

Every board needs some structure for its internal operations. Without structure there is no common reference to rely on when the unexpected happens. Specific standards serve as a guide to do the right thing, particularly when inappropriate board member behavior must be addressed. Standard practices help to provide clarity in dealing with disorder in the boardroom, members who are habitually late, or even with illegible minutes. At the other end of the spectrum, too much structure and too many rules can stifle creativity and cause members to focus more on rules than results.

The most minimal structural element of a business meeting is to start and end on time. Maintaining this piece of structure is the responsibility of the board chair. However, he or she cannot always control the comings and goings of individual board members unless the board culture has already stressed the importance of respecting the meeting's time frame. Board members often are busy people, running from appointment to appointment; or they are parents who must accommodate their children's schedules. It is common courtesy to stick to set time limits, show respect for private time, and allow board members to remain attentive to the rest of their lives.

BOARD STRUCTURE AND THE ROLE OF PARLIAMENTARY ORDER

A large number of nonprofit bylaws mention that board meetings are run according to *Robert's Rules of Order*. This could be seen as a good thing or a bad thing. Without a doubt, the 700 pages of this little red book contain innumerable wisdoms and solutions to many sticky situations. It also spells out the exact steps for just about every boardroom event in detail. If the bylaws stipulate that Mr. Robert determines the board's processes, this notion cannot be selective. Either the rules are followed or the board should clarify its relationship with Robert's Rules in a different manner.

Robert's Rules of Order is the most comprehensive, most widely used reference of meeting manuals. The original edition saw light in 1876; today, it is in its 10th edition. As the name indicates, the rules described in the book are best in a larger parliamentary setting, where the representatives determine what is best for their constituents who elected them to that position to begin with (i.e., government representatives). Each representative does whatever is necessary to get his or her opinion accepted. It is standard and acceptable to represent a specific group and drive that group's agenda. Competition can be fierce between representatives of different opinions. It is important in that setting to follow exact rules and regulations so that everyone is able to interpret the methods of operation in the same manner. Deviations may indicate that one side is being advantaged or disadvantaged. Exact process matters. If process did not exist, it would be easy to contest every unfavorable vote by referring to technicalities that are otherwise deemed unarguable by relying on procedure.

This atmosphere is (or should be) foreign to small nonprofit boards. Board members do not (or should not) act as representatives for a specific section of the organization's constituents and solely advocate its needs. They should certainly bring the understanding, wishes, and preferences of their groups into the boardroom, but only in the form of examples and testimonials of perspectives that the full board must consider when looking at the needs of the constituency at large. This principle does

---

A PARLIAMENTARIAN IN THE BOARDROOM

If a board includes a position for a parliamentarian to police the processes in the boardroom, it is likely taking the strict structure approach and may end up spending precious time on discussing who is allowed to do what and when. If the purpose is to have a member who is able to guide an unwieldy board to respect the business order and provide professional assistance in a procedural situation that seemingly has no solution, a parliamentarian can be of help. If a meeting is very process-oriented (which may be the case in some membership organizations especially), it is possible to retain a parliamentarian to help when necessary. This person does not necessarily need to be an insider of the organization.

not mean that a board member should not have strong *individual* opinions on an issue. A variety of individual opinions bring diversity to the discussion and have an impact on how the final opinion of the *board* is formed. This understanding allows the board to focus on results and not get bogged down by process details as can happen in a true parliamentary setting. It provides flexibility that can be adapted to the culture of a board; it brings the focus on discussion and deliberation rather than structuring every expression into a specific order.

By no means is this to say that structure and certain elements of parliamentary order should be *eliminated* from board meetings. Every meeting needs a frame, defined processes, and order. Without them — no matter how jolly and informal the atmosphere in the boardroom is — oligarchy or chaos is allowed to creep in. All parties might be speaking at the same time, the agenda would be difficult to follow, and the chair could lose control.

To avoid such chaos, at minimum: Check whether a quorum is present; declare the meeting started and adjourned; include motions, along with someone to second the motion; and allow the chair to facilitate discussion and make judgment calls when order is lost or unruly members dominate the floor. It is necessary to create a general understanding of what to do if an impasse happens and board members should be educated about the accepted processes and when they apply. Future chairs need training to keep the team cohesive and to respect others' rights to express differing opinions.

When the chair leads the board through the agenda, the use of basic parliamentary order keeps business moving forward. Using motions, board members can bring in issues for discussion. This facilitates tracking and recording. But when a major discussion is launched, the most flexible and probably productive method is to rely on the chair's skills in facilitation. Deliberation can be guided by the chair with a more free-flowing manner that invites open contemplation and creative solutions. When the chair judges that all opinions have been aired and that the group is ready for a vote, he or she may then put the motions back on the table and record the voting results.

If a board chooses to have a professional meeting reference guidebook, such as *Robert's Rules of Order*, it should first study the inventory of some available books and document and choose the reference that most closely fits the board's comfort level. (Check the Suggested Resources on page 79 for further ideas, and have a task force make a recommendation.) A board should determine what parliamentary order means to it and indicate in the bylaws how it plans to use the reference. To include flexibility in the processes, the bylaws could state that the reference serves as a tool to solve a bottleneck when the board is not able to agree on a process issue through direct communication. Legal counsel should interpret the board's intent. Here is one example:

> In case of an impasse or in a situation that cannot be solved via discussion, the board relies on the guidance of *Robert's Rules of Order* [or another preferred reference of choice].

USING DELIBERATION IN DECISION MAKING

As already discussed, meetings need overall structure. But certain parts of a meeting can benefit from a more freewheeling approach. As seasoned consultant Glenn Tecker recommends, the board chair can announce when the meeting suspends parliamentary rules and moves to deliberation. The chair then guides the discussion without having to incorporate motions and other hierarchical details in the process. When it is clear that the board is ready to make a decision, the chair announces that the deliberation part is over and the regular process takes over.

Deliberation drives good decisions; it is the meat and bones of a meeting. During deliberation, members of the board discuss all sides of an issue. Without a thorough airing of all aspects relating to the issue under discussion, it is difficult to end up with a conclusion that is sound, founded, and fair.

The following is a basic outline for conducting the deliberation process and using deliberation time constructively. The left column outlines the process while the right column provides an example of how deliberation works providing a specific example.

Process	Example
First, define the matter at hand. The issue should be introduced in the most neutral way possible. State the key points, define the issue or dilemma (if one exists), and clarify why this issue is important or why the board needs to address it.	The organization needs a new home: • The staff has outgrown its current office space. • Staff is expected to grow by 10 percent over the next year. • The organization would like to be located closer to downtown.
The chair should then state what needs to be accomplished. If there are no objectives to guide the board, the discussion can easily veer off course and the end result may be lopsided and irrelevant. Define the objectives and make sure that everybody is in agreement on those objectives. There should be no contention on this point if the issue has been properly framed.	The board needs to review the proposals presented by the real estate agent and decide on which property best suits the organization's needs.
Board members then share their opinions. Members should bring up their points of view and add details or major points that seem to be missing or that nobody has thought of before, even if they may seem controversial.	• The rents are much higher closer to town. • Being closer to town makes it easier for staff to attend coalition meetings. • A downtown location will help raise the organization's profile. • The organization may be criticized for moving into a more uptown environment, moving away from its grass-roots origins.

(cont.)

(cont.)

Process	Example
Participants can then propose solutions and options for action. Alternative solutions are needed and will require everyone's feedback.	Set up a task force to: study the proposals; visit the proposed sites; investigate other viable alternatives to a downtown location; plan informal focus group of constituents to discuss location selection.
When the chair feels that the board has addressed all sides of the situation thoroughly — and the members of the board echo that notion — and it seems that a general agreement has been reached, it is time to move into collective decision making. Voting can now take place. However, if the board has been discussing only part of a major topic with no intention of making a decision during that meeting, the chair should table the issue until a later date.	All members agree to establish a task force to further review the options.
If the deliberation does not result in reasonable accord, the chair (who has taken an objective stance) evaluates the situation and proposes that the discussion will continue at the next meeting or as soon as any necessary research has been completed by a committee, task force, or an individual appointed.	

Another approach during deliberation is to rely on so-called *systems thinking*. The chair will identify the issue or problem under discussion. He or she proceeds by posing guiding questions that lead to a better understanding of the ripple effects of various options. Ultimately, it is easier to consider possible actions because the board members have a deeper appreciation of the full implications of the decision.

Using small groups during the deliberation process may also be beneficial. Small groups can more efficiently discuss various aspects of the same issue. The board can divide bigger issues into smaller increments, task the smaller groups with discussing the issue, and then report back to the board with their ideas. Smaller groups also allow for more focused reflection and provide more opportunities for less vocal members to make a contribution to the deliberation process.

Board meeting decisions in no way differ from other decisions individuals make in their own lives. Without an open and careful study of the details that make up a case, one can end up relying on wishful thinking rather than on facts and experience. A diversified board that is able to bring a variety of opinions and expertise into the discussion has a better chance of guiding the organization in the right direction — a responsibility that weighs heavily on every board member's shoulders.

REACHING A UNANIMOUS DECISION

Most nonprofit bylaws indicate that the majority voice of a quorum carries the vote, while issues of special importance may need a supermajority.

Unanimity may be a blessing if it is achieved through a thoughtful process and the question has been analyzed from all sides. But it also comes with caveats and may indicate internal problems. With everyone always in full agreement, it may mean that the board is simply rubberstamping recommendations. It could imply that only the noncontroversial aspects of an issue were aired, nobody took the time to do complete research, or the board is composed of similarly thinking individuals who prefer a one-sided story. If unanimity seems to be a pattern, it may be time to investigate some of the reasons behind it.

SEEKING CONSENSUS

Consensus is another approach for making decisions. Seeking consensus — a general agreement to a proposed idea — is not always well understood because it is a complicated process. It demands a skillful facilitator and requires that the board fully understand the consensus-building process. Consensus building may be the most democratic way of coming to a final accord, although it may not be an easy or quick way to run a board meeting.

The principle of consensus building assumes that all points of view are valid and minority views are incorporated into the discussion. The goal is to find a solution that everyone can accept and is willing to implement. Consensus eliminates the win-or-lose approach of a majority vote because it does not count votes. It takes a more qualitative approach, not forcing a compromise but seeking to eliminate objections. It also encourages alternative thinking and fosters innovative solutions.

During the process, the facilitator presents a proposal and invites all participants to express their concerns or reservations. This input may result in a modification of the proposal, gradually allowing it to become more and more specific. Modification moves from major points to fine-tuning the final agreement. Prioritizing points is a useful way of eliminating unacceptable solutions. Synthesizing opinions brings clarification to concepts. When the facilitator feels that a mutual agreement has been reached, this is articulated and the chair asks if participants agree that the articulated statement accurately reflects the consensus. If there is no objection, it is recorded as the group's decision.

Consensus method may not be practical for all board decisions because of its cumbersome and time-consuming aspect, but it could be used for highly sensitive, risky, or ethical issues that the board must tackle, such as determining a desired profile for the board or deciding on a stand the board wants to take on a controversial environmental issue. A consensus may not always be reached. A small fraction of the board can block action that might be desired by the majority of members. A deadlock may happen if a board member is unwilling or unable to buy the principle of the method itself. In these situations, the objection must be worked out before the proposal can go forward. Ultimately, a totally new approach to the question at hand may be necessary and the full process must start all over again.

BENEFITS AND CHALLENGES OF CONSENSUS DECISION MAKING

Benefits

- Encourages collaborative team work

- Allows board members to get to know each other better

- Respects minority views

- Can be considered a fair process

- Breeds innovation and creativity

- Removes road blocks to implementation

Challenges

- Requires a very skillful facilitator

- Can be a lengthy process

- May lead to diluted solutions

- May end in a deadlock

ELECTING A DEVIL'S ADVOCATE

To push a board into thinking more creatively or to unblock tendencies of stagnation, the board may want to create an official position of a "devil's advocate." By choosing a single member, or rotating the job among board members, the devil's advocate has the role of always asking the questions that nobody else wants to ask, or to purposefully contradict presented arguments. As long as it is understood that this is the intended role of the board member during the meeting, the board can turn the idea into a productive game. No argument should be off limits as long as it does not get personal and it encourages members to consider alternative options. Any exercise that forces a board to open up to accepting new ideas can unleash the sleeping force and turn an ordinary board into a vigorous and insightful group of team members. However, a perennial devil's advocate may eventually test the board's patience, at which time the game becomes counterproductive.

How Do Boards Vote?

In most cases, deliberation (or whatever method the board uses to get ready for decision making or the final agreement) results in a vote. By casting a vote, each board member expresses his or her personal assessment of the situation and thus contributes to collective decision making. However, it is only the collective vote that counts at the end.

Whether a board votes by a showing of hands or by voice is up to the board. The size of the board may determine the method. There is no right or wrong way of voting as long as the secretary is able to count the votes and can ascertain who voted for and who voted against. It is unusual for a board to vote by ballot. Ballots are more common and practical for membership meetings where larger groups are present, and only the final count matters.

Openness is an element of board interaction. This demands that board members trust and understand each other as votes are cast according to their best judgment. Some boards use a secret ballot when electing officers. The purpose of this is to eliminate any adverse impact on relationships when a choice has to be made between two peers. To further eliminate this pressure from officer elections, it may make sense to have the governance committee act as a facilitator for the process. In this case, the governance committee holds discreet conversations with officer candidates outside of the boardroom. Committee members are able to confidentially communicate with officer candidates and other board members and then present for confirmation one candidate who either turned out to be the best choice or an ultimate compromise.

Youth Vote on the Board

It is an excellent idea to bring young people into the boardroom — especially for an organization that deals with youth. Youth bring a different perspective to the table and can enliven board discussions. However, many of the legal and generational issues should be discussed before bringing youth members onto the board and careful board training is necessary to turn this idea into a successful endeavor. The law does not address the soft side of the topic but in most states determines the legal age for voting board members. Most commonly, the law excludes persons younger than 18.

The age limit deals with a young person's right — or capacity — to sign legal documents and thus absorb liability for the organization. Be it a youth or adult, an individual's abilities are often subjective and the law cannot distinguish between them. The law sets an age limit, which usually coincides with the legal age in the state.

A board with young members has options. On the strict side, it is not wise to elect minors as officers who often need special authorities such as signing checks and approving contracts. Young members could also serve as nonvoting members, but that partially defeats the objective. The board could form a separate youth advisory council and ensure that its feedback is seriously considered. Electing youth to committees is another choice. These are ways to keep the youth perspective viable and allow young people to gain experience and leadership skills for future board service.

A few states by now allow nonprofit boards to vote via electronic means but require a clear process to make the vote legally binding. Minnesota is one of the forerunners. In Minnesota, nonprofit boards that choose to use electronic voting must be able to create a record that can be retained, retrieved, and reviewed. Board members must agree in writing to carry out board action without a meeting. It is important to authenticate the actual consent when a vote takes place, as it is always possible for outsiders to log in. Presently at least Texas, Virginia, Wisconsin, Utah, Minnesota, and Washington, DC have endorsed the use of electronically scanned signatures for electronic board meetings. For truly sensitive e-mails, it is possible to encrypt message contents so that only authorized recipients are able to open them. Privacy issues are in danger if proper precautions are not taken.

DECIDING BY MAJORITY RULE

Most state laws require that a majority of the board members present (after a quorum is determined) must agree before a vote is carried. A majority means 51 percent — or, if there are 10 voting members present, six will carry the vote. The justification for this law, again, is to ensure that there is a reasonable agreement among board members on the desired outcomes of a vote.

Majority rule usually refers to normal board decisions. Bylaws should distinguish between "normal" and "extraordinary" decisions. They should clarify what kinds of major resolutions — ones that have a foremost impact on the board or the entire organization — should require a greater than majority vote. A small part of the board should not be able to decide whether to shut down the organization, approve a merger, amend the articles of incorporation or the bylaws, fire the chief executive, or remove a board member or an officer. It is common to require a two-thirds or three-quarters vote on these issues.

A board could also agree ahead of time on what kinds of decisions demand deliberation, when a simple majority is enough, or when the board must rely on a higher level of agreement. For example:

- A conceptual amendment to a bylaws clause must be discussed and a supermajority must pass it.

- To confirm a new address in the same document is a technicality; this proposal can be included in the consent agenda and voted by majority rule.

- Firing a chief executive should be deliberated by the full board with a high degree of consent needed.

- Deciding to use an executive search firm can be determined by a majority.

VOTING BY PROXY

State law often defines whether a nonprofit board may use proxy votes. A proxy generally refers to either the person with a power of attorney, or the piece of paper that conveys this power to vote or make decisions on behalf of a board member in his or her absence. This practice is commonly used by for-profit corporations and nonprofit membership organizations during membership meetings. Under those circumstances it can be highly beneficial and useful as it allows for adequate representation when the reality of bringing together thousands of shareholders or members is out of the question and impractical. However, for nonprofit boards, proxy voting is generally not a good practice.

State laws that address this issue agree with this notion. Why? A board member is accountable for his or her own actions on the board. Because of liability issues, the board member is not in a good position to delegate major responsibilities to someone else. A board member must adhere to the duty of care; thus, that careful decision making is more than simply deciding to vote yes or no.

Most board decisions *are not* simple yes or no votes. If that were the case, it would be easy to share basic documents with board members and ask them to indicate whether they were for or against the issue. So why even bother to come to the meeting? Because it is impossible to know ahead of time what the true issues are in the minds of the other board members. During deliberation a point may come up that could turn the tables around. A board member indicating opposition to a proposal in a proxy might change his or her mind after hearing the arguments. A proxy can lock a vote in prematurely.

Managing Split Votes

If board members regularly feel incompatible and divisive, there must be an underlying systemic reason. Few boards are unanimous all the time — and if they were, it would leave room for question.

For small boards, a constant split vote may indicate that the board cannot absorb differing opinions. One or two individuals veering off the main stream can create a split vote. The solution may be to elevate board member recruitment to the top of the board's priority list. This will help to build a larger member base that can contribute to information sharing and that is able to analyze all questions carefully.

If a board is plagued by power struggles and cliques, divisiveness is an automatic consequence. Private agendas often guide members' opinions and winning a debate becomes the objective. Board members can forget that they are part of an important team, whose role is to lead the organization forward. Differing opinions can be a blessing during a deliberation process, but working toward a consensus or a compromise is also part of a democratic process. If cliques or competing factions define the board composition, it may be necessary to eliminate this obstacle. If board members are not able to solve this serious problem on their own, it may be valuable to invite an outside facilitator to help iron out the stumbling block and make use of conflict resolution techniques.

Occasional split votes are to be expected. This can happen with controversial issues or when the topic simply has not yet been researched or analyzed thoroughly. It can also happen when board members simply react with their deep personal conviction concerning an issue or when a personal experience does not allow them to deviate from their initial perspective. Additional time or work on the issue may be all that is needed or the chair may attempt to rephrase the debated issue to make it more palatable and acceptable to more board members.

Without having to rely on the chair to break a tie (see page 41 for "Should the Chair Vote?"), a more constructive approach would be to test different decision-making processes that have been outlined earlier in this chapter. Even if a board's bylaws require a majority rule to carry the vote, the board may benefit from trying the following:

- Encourage more early information sharing.

- Attempt consensus building with the board.

- Restate the issue using different words.

- Ask all board members to carefully elaborate on the obstacles that they see ahead of them and what measures would turn the issue around in their minds.

All of these efforts assume that board members place personal needs in proper perspective and understand and accept their collective role in defining what the organizational needs are.

CHOOSING NOT TO VOTE

Do board members have the right — the moral right — not to express their opinion when no apparent conflicting or logistical reason exists? Should board members ever shy away from controversial or otherwise tough decisions? Is voting an obligation or a privilege in the boardroom setting? These are challenging questions and it is difficult to propose a stock answer.

While abstention is usually tied to a conflict of interest, sometimes board members do not vote because they remain undecided (often corrected by further discussion). In some cases, a board member may not want to cast an unpopular vote or vote against another peer. This could be construed as having "undue" influence or voting with the pack. Rubberstamping boards often let strong leaders guide their opinions.

Abstention can produce two kinds of results: It can prevent a majority from carrying the vote, or it can allow the final decision to swing to the other side because of lack of sufficient and determined support. If a board is clearly divided and time allows it, the best solution may be to table the issue until the next meeting and assign a task force to continue work in between.

5.
Meeting Participation

A good board is made up of a diverse group of people, involving many differences that especially include varying personality traits. People can be either extroverts or introverts, articulate or tongue-tied, passionate or unconcerned, altruistic or selfish. Board members are there for different reasons and possess differing skills. Some may be there to learn more, while others may feel all they can do is teach others. Some focus on the little details and others see the big picture. Some are team players and others highly individualistic. Unfortunately, some may have private agendas and are self-absorbed. All of these qualities and characteristics — and many others — must work together or the board will spend an inordinate time solving communication problems and unnecessary misunderstandings.

This chapter looks at the people who make up a board meeting along with guidelines for their participation in the meeting process: rules for meeting attendance, managing improper boardroom behavior, conflicts of interest, and private agendas.

Participants can animate a board meeting or cause it to drag on interminably. Some attendees should be present from beginning to end and others appear only at critical moments. Some participants lead the show in the meeting room; others prepare for the meeting before and after. Clarifying the expectations of every person affiliated with a board meeting simply ensures that unnecessary confusion is absent and that the right individuals are chosen for the appropriate roles.

A board member

- wants to feel that his or her time has been well spent and contributions were appreciated.

- wants to see that the chair conducts the meeting in a capable manner and that other members express valid and relative comments to the issue under discussion.

- wants to get excited about the work and the accomplishments of the organization and leave invigorated and with anticipation of the next meeting.

The chair

- wants an orderly meeting with active participants.

- welcomes unconventional comments that stimulate discussion and force even the quiet ones to express their opinions.

- wants to follow the agenda and expects clear and committed decisions at the end.

The chief executive

- wants a board that understands the challenges with which he or she must struggle every day.

- wants to feel that the board is behind him or her, supporting efforts and providing clear and unambiguous guidance for future actions.

How to consolidate all these expectations? By looking at all the aspects that influence the atmosphere and desired outcomes of the meeting, it is possible to start isolating the factors that make this possible.

First and foremost, it is important to acknowledge the fact that board members ultimately validate a meeting. Quorum requirements alone spell out the necessity of their presence. If there is no quorum, the legal requirements are not met. The room may be filled with guests and honorary members but, without the voting power present, it is simply a gathering or an assembly of interested individuals who cannot take action. Without board members, there would be no other aspects of participation left to discuss.

MEETING ATTENDANCE REQUIREMENTS

It is not an exaggeration to say that meeting attendance is obligatory. When a person accepts an invitation to serve on a board, his or her number one obligation is to come to meetings. Additionally, board service comes with the caveat of personal liability, which involves prudent and independent decision making. Without discussion and informed voting, a board member is not acting as a fiduciary for the organization. Absence endangers a member's capacity to both be educated and to inform others, and it can be risky.

Simple presence, unfortunately, does not suffice. Active participation should also be considered obligatory. Counting heads and meeting quorum requirements allows the board to function within the legal parameters. But, as already mentioned, legality builds a necessary framework and gives the board the permission to act; it does not provide wisdom and ultimate personal accountability. Involvement in deliberation (asking questions, providing feedback, sharing ideas, or refusing to accept easy solutions) builds the needed base for wise decisions. After all, is that not the purpose for coming together?

WHAT IS A QUORUM?

A quorum defines how many board members must be in the room before a meeting can begin. No board meeting can take place without a quorum. If there is no quorum, the group that has gathered cannot make decisions and must adjourn and schedule its next meeting. Many state laws set a quorum as a majority of voting board members if the bylaws do not define other standards. If the bylaws mention nothing about a quorum, then state law prevails. Quorum *should*, however, make an appearance in the bylaws.

Why is a quorum required? Consider the following situation: A board with nine members has a meeting set for a Thursday evening. It is a stormy night and only the chair and another officer manage to come to the meeting. The two vote to remove three of their fellow members and assign to themselves a signature authority for all checks over $200.

This is an exaggerated example, but it makes a point: A quorum ensures that one or just a few board members do not make decisions without the board's consent.

It is always useful to contemplate the worst-case scenarios when defining decision-making quorum standards for the board. Combining a bad quorum definition with a majority rule can also spell disaster. For example, a board with 16 members and a 40 percent quorum requirement means that a minimum of six people is required for a vote. In this case, four members can determine the fate of an issue.

Some boards having difficulties with board member absenteeism may consider lowering the quorum because without one it is simply too difficult to come to final decisions. This is an approach that, ultimately, tries to correct a bad situation with a worse remedy, sending the wrong message to members about their obligation to attend meetings. Boards that set the quorum at 100 percent, hoping to ensure full representation, may find themselves in the same dilemma because, oftentimes, at least one member is absent from a meeting for a good reason.

THE ABSENTEE BOARD MEMBER

It is only natural that from time to time a board member will miss a meeting. When this happens, the member should communicate the excuse to the chair. It is inappropriate to just not show up. If members have marked the year's meeting dates in their calendars, only exceptional and unavoidable excuses should be acceptable: illness, family misfortune, or logistical causes beyond a member's control. When missing a meeting is unavoidable, it may be possible to participate via teleconference.

ADDRESSING ABSENCE FROM MEETINGS IN THE BYLAWS

Be aware of clauses in the bylaws concerning absenteeism. Some bylaws automatically consider a board member resigned after missing a certain number of meetings during a year or consecutively. Below are some sample bylaws clauses. Consider what kind of phrasing is appropriate for your board.

1. Any elected officer or board member who is absent from two (2) consecutive regular meetings during a single administrative year shall automatically vacate the seat and vacancy shall be filled as provided by the bylaws. However, the board considers each absence as a separate circumstance and may expressly waive such absence by affirmative vote of a majority of its members.

2. Absence from three (3) consecutive board meetings within a fiscal year without excuse is equivalent to resignation from the board. Confirmation of such absences and subsequent removal shall be given to the board member in writing by the secretary of the board.

3. Any director may be removed by a two-thirds (2/3) vote of a quorum whenever, in the board's judgment, the best interest of the corporation would be served. Notice of the removal shall be given in writing to the board member by the secretary not more than ten (10) days subsequent to such action.

4. Board members who miss two (2) consecutive meetings shall be asked to resign.

A prolonged absence or missing several meetings in a row deserves attention. Probably the most common reason for board members to regularly miss meetings is lack of interest — their concern is just no longer there. The member may feel that he or she has done all that is possible. However, these feelings can be very difficult to communicate. The board member may feel like giving up or that he or she is letting others down. When a board member starts missing meetings, it is up to the chair to pick up the phone and simply ask: "What's up?" If the reason is the one described above, the call may just be the saving grace. This is an opportunity for the disinterested individual to explain why he or she has lost interest or to communicate why he or she is too busy to continue. If there is no way to turn the situation around, the chair may need to ask the board member to officially resign. This is the most civilized way to handle a perfectly natural situation. It provides a dignified way out while reserving the possibility to keep the person involved in another capacity that does not require the same commitment.

By contacting a missing board member, the chair may learn that there are personal problems that have prevented regular attendance. The reason may be health related, a family matter, or a delicate, private subject that the board member may not even want to divulge. In this situation, the chair is often asked to demonstrate special sensitivity and skills in dealing with the situation in the most appropriate manner possible. Trust may be the key to reach the right solution and confidentiality is crucial. Sometimes the right approach is to ask the board member to resign for the time being and, if the situation improves, made to feel welcome to apply for board membership again.

If the reason for absence is a bad match between the member and the board, or that the expectations of the job were far different than the realities, the chair should request an official resignation. The chair may also wish to remain in touch in order to perhaps involve this person in the mission via other methods.

If the reasons for absence are uninspiring meetings or failure to use or take advantage of the skills of the member, the chair will hopefully get the message. There is a danger of possibly losing a valuable board member because the board was not functioning up to par. The chair should be able to listen and validate the board member's concerns and make the necessary efforts to correct the problems.

Logistics, as discussed previously, can also be a reason for low attendance. Be it transportation issues, child-care needs, timing of the meetings, or other reasons, the easiest way to solve this problem is to allow board members to bring it out in the open before it turns into an obstacle. Transportation and child care can be arranged and meeting schedules can often be adjusted. By simply presenting them to the board, many other practical issues may be easily and creatively worked out.

Some boards, either as a precautionary measure or by being confronted with a situation, draft policies concerning leaves of absence. Should a board consider temporary absence acceptable or should it deal with the issue more strictly? Requests for leave may warrant thorough consideration by the board. A board member may need to be absent for several months due to health issues or travel obligations and be unable to attend meetings or fulfill other board responsibilities. At least two options are available: 1) The board may request that the member resign while still allowing him or her to reapply for service when the situation has cleared itself, or 2) the board may have a policy that allows members to take a leave of absence under dire circumstances and relieves them of duties for the necessary period.

If the latter option is the choice, both the board and the board member in question need to ensure that proper precautions are set in place. The board may want to draft a policy that specifically states the acceptable circumstances for a leave of absence. Automatic sabbaticals are not a good idea, as they undermine the basic commitment of board service. Weariness or other distractions should not warrant a review of the case. The minutes must reflect the dates of absence in order to protect the board member from liability. Keep the member informed about what happened during his or her absence by sharing documents, minutes, and board resolutions. This is a cautionary measure meant to bring the member up to date on board business before returning to service. A vigilant board member might check with his or her own legal counsel of possible considerations that otherwise may go unnoticed. Only a lawyer can assess whether all liability issues have been addressed in the agreement.

THE BOARD CHAIR

It is difficult to imagine an efficient meeting without a designated facilitator or leader. During board meetings this role usually falls on the shoulders of the chair. (When the chair is not available, the vice chair steps in. Running the meeting in the absence of the chair is one of the main duties of a vice chair but the board may also elect a temporary or *pro tem* chair.) However, there is no law that says that the chair must preside over the meeting, even if the title seems to indicate so. If the chair is brilliant in all other ways but simply runs a lousy meeting, the board may consider assigning this task to someone else. Doing so may indicate a lack of confidence in the chair because a leader is expected to demonstrate leadership qualities. As the person in charge, the rest of the board expects the chair to be articulate, decisive, and in total control of all situations. But it does not make sense to sacrifice the quality of the meeting simply because of tradition. A board should choose the best facilitator, and with luck, that person is the chair.

The role of the chair (we assume here that the board chair is presiding) is to make sure that the agenda fits the meeting and that the meeting runs smoothly. The chair ensures that board members are assuming their roles and responsibilities. During the meeting the chair facilitates the proceedings and discussion, and guards dignity during the debate. This demands a basic knowledge of the parliamentary order, even if the board does not adhere to strict parliamentary procedure. The chair also is expected to have completed the necessary preparations for addressing the big issues of the meeting without having decided ahead of time what the outcome should be. All of these expectations mean that the chair has the skill to engage every member in the discussion — tame the wild ones and encourage the quiet ones.

It is up to the chair to ensure that the objectives in the agenda are achieved. A good agenda allows for some flexibility and a skillful chair knows when to utilize that flexibility. If one of the main issues simply demands more attention than anticipated, the chair should judge whether the discussion should continue or if it is advisable to keep to the schedule and send the issue to committee for further study, bringing it back at the next meeting.

The chair's role does not end when the meeting does. There must be continued communication with the chief executive and with board members who are assigned special tasks. The chair is in the best position — better than the chief executive — to check on peers and ensure that everyone will come back with the appropriate work done. As a good practice, the chair can make a quick call or send an e-mail a few weeks prior to the next meeting to check on the status of the assignments. The chair can also contact board members who missed the last meeting, sending a message that the chair cares and wants every member present every time.

Board meetings follow a continual cycle, leaving little rest for the board chair. The position of board chair is not limited to a call to order and adjournment. It involves regular preparation and follow-up, and takes a special commitment to the other members of the board — and the job itself.

STAYING FOCUSED ON THE RIGHT ISSUES

Disorderly and unstructured discussions can often be attributed to the chair's lack of skills. The chair has the gavel — literally or figuratively — to guide the discussion and participants. A good facilitator is able to keep the participants in line, engaged, and interested; follow the agenda; assess when additional time allowance for a topic is warranted; and determine when the issue has been sufficiently discussed. The chair also directs the cadence and content of the debate.

Many boards include members who have a need to perform. They must comment on every question. If the chair is not able to limit their delivery, the direction of the discussion can become lopsided, steering the board off on a tangent that may not be relevant or that receives exaggerated attention. To correct this, the chair may want to develop rules for how long every board member may speak. The board might want to elect a timekeeper or another member who raises a red flag when time is up. The chair can also limit the number of times a board member may speak during the meeting in order to leave time for the quieter members or those who need more time to think before expressing their opinions.

The chair must also be able to determine when everything has been said and it is time to vote. Or, if it is impossible to reach consensus, the chair has the right to table the discussion, if the issue allows, and bring it back during the next session after tempers have cooled and additional data are available. In this situation, the chair's decisiveness and good judgment allow the meeting to proceed.

The best tool for the chair to maintain focus on the debate is the agenda. The agenda is the recipe for the meeting, and including the appropriate and timely issues in the agenda can eliminate irrelevance. However, a carefully planned board meeting agenda must be flexible. The chair and the chief executive may need to turn the tables around and restructure the meeting altogether on short notice or, at least, insert a vital item between regular issues. This reflects responsibility and responsiveness and communicates to the rest of the board that they are on top of the issues.

SHOULD THE CHAIR VOTE?

Many boards struggle with the question of whether the board chair should vote during the meeting. Let's not forget that voting rights do extend to the chair, as he or she has the same rights as every other board member. It is up to each individual board chair to determine how he or she wants to use this right. As the facilitator of the meeting, the chair potentially has a chance to influence the free flow of opinions or ensure that a particular angle gets preferred visibility. The chair's vote can be very influential and all the more impacts the power of his or her position. It is important that the chair remains impartial during deliberation, without promoting his or her own opinion during facilitation. But at the end, the chair may simply vote with the rest of the board members. Should the chair have a particularly strong opinion on an issue, he or she may choose to temporarily delegate the role of facilitator to another board member while discussion takes place. This enables the chair to contribute to the discussion and offer important insight and direction without appearing to sway the discussion in a particular direction. Some chairs choose to vote only to avoid or break a tie. Others never vote. For the most part, the chair automatically casts his or her vote at the end of the debate.

THE CHIEF EXECUTIVE

When term limits are enforced effectively, board members come and go. The chief executive, however, can stay with the organization for many years and holds the organizational memory, often acting as the partaker who keeps an eye on the revolving door — many times left to deal with the consequences. Board work and meetings evolve as new members enter the scene. The chief executive is in a good position to monitor the change and use his or her influence in bringing new members up to speed and familiarizing them with the existing processes. At the same time, when tested methods seem outdated and need refurbishment, it is necessary to listen to new ideas and implement them as is feasible.

In most nonprofits, the chief executive is not a voting member of the board — an issue that every board must discuss in order to define its own relationship with the staff leader. Voting rights, however, should not affect the role the chief executive plays at board meetings. **The chief executive is an essential key figure in ensuring that the board is well equipped to make the best possible decisions and govern the organization with commitment.** If this concept is actively nurtured, accepted, and embraced by individual board members, the chief executive is in an extremely powerful position to drive the organization with full backing by the board.

Benefits of KPAWN Meetings

One way that the board can show support for the chief executive is to install regular minimeetings with him or her in an executive session, either before or at the end of every board meeting. These sessions are called KPAWN, or what Keeps the President Awake at Night meetings. In only a quarter of an hour, allow the chief executive to talk about issues that are his or her biggest concerns at the moment. These topics may cover funding problems, staff retention, burnout fears, or even more personal pressures, but they all have an impact on daily work life. Divulging these important issues without fear of judgment or worry gives the leader a chance to both release some pressure in a more informal setting and discuss situations that do not necessarily belong in the official meeting agenda. Naturally, the chief executive must use good judgment when choosing the issues that are shared with the board in order not to invite the board to micromanage or make decisions on his or her behalf. These sessions also allow the board members to understand and appreciate the stress factor that every nonprofit chief executive knows much too well.

In reality, only a few board meetings would probably succeed or even take place if it were not for the chief executive. As the chair often takes the role of the spiritual leader and the manager of internal board member relations, the chief executive is the force behind organizing the actual meeting. He or she prepares the agenda along with the chair, provides an invaluable perspective and background clarity to the issues to which the board must pay attention, ensures that all the logistics for the meeting are carefully executed, coordinates the production and distribution of board packets, and ultimately stands behind the meeting figuratively and structurally.

Naturally, the chief executive's planning and communication with the board chair form the foundation for effective meetings. Few would deny the importance of this partnership for the overall success of the organization but, in order for the partnership to be effective, these two leaders must feel comfortable with the division of

ABSENCE OF THE CHIEF EXECUTIVE AT A BOARD MEETING

It is meeting time again. As long as quorum is reached, the meeting can proceed. If the chief executive is a nonvoting member, whether or not he or she is present does not affect the quorum. However, as the chief executive is such an important figure in the meeting, his or her absence would be unfortunate.

In the case where the chief executive cannot attend the meeting, the board chair should take it upon him or herself to communicate with the executive afterwards and provide good feedback on what happened at the meeting. If there are some decisions on the table that would absolutely require the chief executive's input or greatly benefit from it, the board might either include the executive via teleconference, or if possible, postpone the discussion or final decision until the next meeting.

labor. While both are partners in planning, the chief executive is *accountable* to the full board and the chair is the contact and *representative* of the full body.

A wise chief executive does not tell the board what to do nor does he or she have the authority to do so. The executive does the necessary homework that helps justify to the board why certain issues are critical and demand priority or overall attention. This happens by giving the board the right information in the right format, whether it is in the chief executive's report, included in the board packet, or inserted into materials sent to members in between meetings. Avoiding detailed daily accounts of what happens in the office eliminates the detailed inquisition so typical of micromanaging boards. The chief executive proves to the board that the board's work matters when it sees that its directives have been implemented, the organization is well managed, and results are positive.

The chief executive should also remain active in suggesting and planning ways to educate board members and build their capacity. A wise executive works with the board to identify what information the board needs on a regular basis in order to provide appropriate and effective oversight.

STAFF

Very few board meetings take place without staff present. Naturally, the chief executive is indispensable but many of the staff members have roles to play, too. It is important to remember, however, that board meetings are business meetings for board members; they are not meetings to focus on the administrative and managerial concerns of the staff. Staff meetings exist separately for that purpose.

The staff has the expertise to carry out the board's directives to the organization. If the chief executive has hired the right people, there is a pool of capable individuals who can give the board needed perspective on big issues that appear on the agenda: The chief financial officer knows the intricacies of the budget and the financial statements and is the best choice to answer board members' questions on those documents; the development director has the latest information on fundraising efforts as well as feedback from major funders; the program and marketing directors can clarify the gains or struggles of key program or sales efforts; and the president's report, already included in the consent agenda, should contain highlights of the recent trends, often making it unnecessary for chief staff members to make additional reports unless a special focus will be placed on one of their areas of responsibility. The staff's main role at the meeting is to be available for consultation and to support the chief executive.

Staff members rarely need to sit in the room through the entire board meeting. The agenda should spell out when specific issues are being discussed and when staff members should be present. Equally, the chair or the chief executive can indicate when staff's assistance is no longer needed. If a meal is served at a meeting, staff may be invited to join the board. This allows board members to get to know senior staff — or, if feasible, the entire staff — in a more relaxed setting.

Some boards regularly invite all staff members to sit through the meeting. The purpose, most likely, is to eliminate any concerns about secrecy and fears about the board making decisions that are not well-founded and debated. This practice may not be practical for most organizations as it has implications for the effective use of staff time and the meeting space may not accommodate the full staff. A well-organized chief executive, under all circumstances, debriefs the staff after a board meeting. BoardSource, for example, regularly has a staff meeting scheduled closely following the board meeting. It allows the chief executive to communicate with all staff members about the board's reaction to presented issues and to explain new guidelines or directives that the board specifically articulated for the next quarter or the remainder of the year.

If senior staff members are invited to directly report to the board, respect their expertise and invite them to sit at the table. When staff is providing necessary feedback and background information during a meeting, the board is using them as advisors. It is, however, necessary to be clear about their respective function and clarify the reason for the invitation. If this is not done, confusion about roles may lead to staff dominating the discussion. If the board has an open-door policy for all staff — as controversial as this practice may be — nonparticipating staff members do not belong around the table but should have separate seats at the periphery.

OUTSIDERS AND GUESTS

In addition to board members and staff, there are a variety of other people who might be present during a board meeting. What brings these individuals to the meeting depends on their possible contributions to the session, certain legal stipulations, their concern for the organization, or the overall attitude of the board that encourages outsiders. Or, looking at them from a slightly different point of view, they are either invited by the board, self-invited, or they serve a standard role during the meeting. It is important that everyone is aware of who is in the room and what each individual's role is.

Speakers and experts on specific issues under board examination are common guests of board meetings. It makes sense to bring in an outside opinion or perspective when the board is dealing with major strategic issues. Examples of these speakers might include: an industry specialist who can introduce the board to field-specific questions that must be understood before setting new policy; a statistician or a pollster with data that can help open the board's eyes when new directions are being reviewed; a marketing expert to guide the board on communications issues if staff does not carry this expertise. These guests often stay only for the time when their assistance is needed or they may come as a luncheon speaker and extend the stay over to a more informal discussion afterwards.

The board may invite a lawyer (or sometimes a parliamentarian) to join a meeting when particularly tricky issues are being handled. It is better not to engage a board member who is a lawyer for this task if the counsel ends up representing the board or the organization in a legal matter.

Equally, the board may invite an outside accountant to a meeting when specific financial issues are a concern. Naturally, there needs to be an annual meeting with the auditor. This is the board's opportunity to discuss the financial statements and the overall financial practices — internal controls, processes, policies, and staff's capacity — in an executive session without any staff present.

Many boards have nonvoting members who serve in an advisory capacity and may have an open invitation to participate in meetings. These members may be former board members or chairs, representatives from affiliates or supporting organizations, or liaisons from advisory groups.

Special meetings may be organized and run by facilitators or consultants as well. Depending on their purpose, these guests may simply steer the board through a process or guide and provide input in decision making. Self-assessment, strategic planning, or preparation for a capital campaign may cause the board to engage an outside consultant.

Sometimes funders want to observe a board meeting to get a better understanding of how the board functions, what its goals are, and how it meets those goals. Or, funders may be invited to come to see how the board demonstrates a readiness in undertaking a new endeavor or to continue the present course that may be specifically dear to that funder.

Constituents may demand an opportunity to deliver a communiqué to the board or otherwise have a chance to monitor closely the organization's governance processes and decisions. Customers and clients may also be asked to come and give a testimony of how they have benefited from the organization. These testimonies can have a powerful effect on the motivation of board members, and the board meeting is a perfect venue for encouraging the full board as a group.

Boards functioning under sunshine laws do not have the luxury to plan outsiders' attendance. If the meetings are open to the public, anyone interested may be in the room. As already discussed in Chapter 1, it is acceptable and desirable to communicate behavioral rules and process details to observers. Experience may gradually train the meeting organizers to anticipate the size of the observing crowd or, when particularly controversial or otherwise tricky issues are on the published agenda, it is better to be prepared for vocal guests.

If the board does not have to follow sunshine laws, outsiders should be admitted by invitation only. When issues discussed in the boardroom are not yet ready for public discussion or otherwise need to be handled confidentially, the board can always retreat to an executive session if the situation so requires. Logistically it is helpful for the staff to know how many people are going to be present and what other arrangements may be needed. Without a policy or a procedure for inviting guests, under some circumstances, either divisive or negligent board members may willingly or accidentally create situations that are difficult to manage or that create undue stress for staff.

It is not uncommon to find boards that openly invite outsiders to come to their meetings. These boards often have a particularly strong sense for transparency and need for sending a message that there are absolutely no secrets within the organization and its leaders. When this message is so openly communicated, the guests also tend to accommodate and simply appreciate the opportunity to observe the board in action.

ORGANIZATIONAL MEMBERS

Membership organizations should have a clear understanding of state laws as they pertain to their members' legal access to documents, financial data, and board meetings. Many state statutes provide members of a nonprofit with the explicit right to inspect minutes and other books and records. Confidential donor information is not included. However, inspection must be for proper purposes, in good faith, and not for feeding individual curiosity or for blackmail purposes.

Whether members have easy access to the boardroom or not, it is imperative for members to understand their relationship to the board. In many cases, the membership elects the board, and this body is the governing body for the organization and holds the fiduciary responsibility in its hands. Membership organizations serve the members who as such have considerable power to approve major organizational decisions. The board may be obligated to seek membership approval on major resolutions. This does not mean that members have the right to second-guess every board decision or have a say in all aspects of governance. By electing the right board members, organizational members have already exercised their right to influence the organization's internal affairs.

BOARD MEMBER CANDIDATES

Inviting board member candidates to attend board meetings may not necessarily be the best way for the governance committee, or the rest of the board, to determine whether he or she is a good prospect. But it can certainly give the candidates an opportunity to judge whether the board is a good fit for them. By observing the board in action, the candidates are able to determine how efficient and focused it is, whether it spends time on important issues or gets caught in administrative details, and whether or not they can get a good sense of the atmosphere in the boardroom. These observations can influence the prospects' opinions to either accept the invitation or to stay as far away from the board as possible!

Keeping Civility in the Boardroom

Sometimes, board members let their emotions take over and allow personal differences to come before important issues. Emotion, in and of itself, is not condemnable by any means. It often reflects the deep passion and concern that a board member has for the organization's mission and work. Particularly, when the organization works with children, animals, the environment, and other social issues, some board members tend to fight for their personal convictions in the boardroom. When emotions are directed at fellow members in a negative manner, private wrangling can divert the focus from what the team is supposed to be doing.

Civility in the boardroom indicates that board members understand and accept the idea that differing opinions are to be treasured, welcomed, and encouraged. Members need to know how to listen and let their peers express their opinions, no matter how esoteric or impossible they may seem, and to respect each other's points of view. Certainly debates can become heated, especially when an issue is controversial, delicate, contentious, troublesome, or touchy. The chair should be careful to look for the signs that the discussion may be getting out of hand and take necessary measures to keep the situation under control.

Difficult board members: Few boards are unfamiliar with this phenomenon. If a board member dominates discussion and seems to have all the answers ready immediately, the chair must find a moment to intercept and turn the "faucet" off. Some boards may need to follow a more structured process in this case and respect a certain level of parliamentary order. This makes it easier for the chair to control the floor and grant individual members the opportunity to take their turn.

Tips: How To Keep the Boardroom Civil

- Arrive on time; stay until the end.

- Come prepared to the meeting. Read meeting materials ahead of time.

- Determine basic ground rules for the meetings.

- Don't use judgmental statements.

- Talk about issues, not people.

- Don't all speak at once.

- Don't criticize those who are absent.

- Don't monopolize the conversation.

- Ask questions to clarify information. There are no stupid questions.

- Keep confidential information confidential.

- Talk about board issues in the boardroom, not afterwards in the parking lot.

- Recognize when there is a conflict of interest and disclose it to the group.

If a board member uses improper language, verbally insults or ridicules fellow members, or otherwise attacks someone personally, the situation should be stopped right away. If immediate change does not occur and the member does not apologize for the language or the comment, he or she may be asked to leave the room. Disagreeing with someone's comments or arguments is perfectly normal, but inappropriate personal behavior in a professional setting should not be accepted. If abusive and misdirected behavior continues, the board may want to consider removing the offending member from the board.

Racist and other ethnic comments, intolerance of other members' personal convictions, and impugning the motives of others should all be considered unacceptable in the boardroom. Whether the comments are intentional or out of ignorance, they deserve immediate attention. After clarifying the problem with the board member, the chair should then consider whether some diversity training is in order for the board.

If a board member has a personal problem relating to excessive alcohol or other substance abuse, and it spills over negatively to his or her board service, the chair or another trusted peer should discuss the issue privately with the member.

Whether dire behaviors are unintentional or deliberate, they divert the board's attention and energies in the wrong direction, and waste valuable time. Boards with problematic members may be able to learn some helpful tips and solutions for dealing with their problems by speaking with members from other boards.

MANAGING CONFLICTS OF INTEREST

The affiliations, interests, and business relationships of active board members may also impact the decisions and transactions of the boards on which they serve. This can be particularly true if there is an overlap between the issues a member deals with in his or her private life and those the board is addressing. This is a fairly common situation and the key is how the board manages the conflict.

Uninfluenced and independent decision making is of primary importance for every board member. Private objectives, personal benefit, or private inurement should not be the driving force when members of the board discuss the internal business of the organization. Board members must rely on their own conscience when deciding what the best action for the organization is; thus, bringing back the old concept of duty of loyalty, which is one of the legal obligations that individual board members must embrace. When serving on a board, a member's loyalties should first lie with the organization's mission and constituency.

When faced with a conflict of interest, the board's only safe harbor is addressing the issue effectively and directly. If the board already has a conflict-of-interest policy, take time to reevaluate its contents:

- Is it clear what constitutes a conflict of interest?

- Who is affected by the policy?

- Who are disqualified individuals on the board and staff?

- What are the steps to eliminating a conflict of interest when the board discusses and votes on issues?

- Whose role is it to enforce the policy?

If the policy clearly states that a board member with a conflict of interest is not allowed to vote or participate in the discussion and will be asked to leave the room, the board is obligated to enforce the policy. This is how a board shows accountability and is able to prove that its decision-making process is intact.

Asking board members to sign a disclosure form at the beginning of each year helps to create an atmosphere of openness. The purpose of the form is to have each board member list possible points of conflict during the coming year. The list should include financial, business, and personal affiliations that might somehow affect the board member's capacity to make untainted judgments. Each ultimate case is situation specific; every potential conflict of interest must be addressed on a case-by-case basis. By creating a preliminary list of conflicts ahead of time, the chair can keep an eye on eventual sticky points. If new conflicts arise during the year, it is expected that a board member in question step forward and recuse him- or herself from the case.

If a board member "forgets" to bring up a conflict-of-interest issue during a board meeting, it is up to the chair to address it. Likewise, if someone else on the board is aware of the conflict, but the chair is not, it is up to the individual to share the information with the chair. Some tact is necessary. If there is a disagreement on the facts or how the conflict presents itself, the full board can be asked to make the ultimate decision.

BRINGING PRIVATE AGENDAS INTO THE BOARDROOM

Private agendas may inhibit some board members from demonstrating their undivided loyalty to the organization. What is a private agenda? A private agenda is personal interests, preferences, or goals that divert the focus of a board member from the organizational issue to that of a private matter. For instance: A board member proposes the creation of a program that benefits his or her child; a board member lobbies for the recruitment of a new member who backs his or her vision for a future direction or action; or a member has aspirations for a leadership role and gradually manages to manipulate and create an inner clique in favor of his or her platform.

In fact, a private agenda is pure conflict of interest and may hover close to private inurement or private benefit. Private agendas do not belong in the boardroom and it is the responsibility of fellow board members to bring the issue to the attention of the chair if the chair is not already aware of it. It is the chair's job to remind all members of their duty of care and loyalty to the mission and to the organization. These duties can be respected only by objective and unbiased decision making.

6.
Other Kinds of Meetings

This book would be incomplete without the discussion of meetings board members are required to attend *outside* of the traditional board meeting. Meetings are simply a part of the way board work gets accomplished. Whether it is the very first meeting of the board, the board's annual meeting, or regular committee meetings, this chapter defines the purposes for these other kinds of meetings. Also included in this chapter is a discussion of membership meetings, the role of the executive committee in special sessions, and the value of holding executive sessions.

FIRST MEETING OF THE FOUNDING BOARD

There is a first for everything, including board meetings. In fact, the first board meeting is of great importance as it brings the board together *officially* for the first time and sets the tone for future meetings. The founder(s) may have brought potential board members together several times before — individually or as a group — but the first official meeting is the founding meeting of the organization. Any previous get-togethers most likely have been informal gatherings or communications to kick off the planning period or to become better acquainted socially.

During the first meeting, the board will need to approve the purpose of the organization. It has a task to elect officers and grant them needed authority to act on behalf of the organization. This may include the right to sign checks and organizational documents, open bank accounts, or represent the board or the organization when necessary. If the bylaws have not yet been written, this meeting should start the process. The board should assign the job of creating the first draft of the bylaws to an individual or a task force. All other necessary procedures relating to the formation of the nonprofit can also be accomplished by committee or task force. Depending on the type of nonprofit the group is creating, task forces may be formed to research and acquire the necessary licenses, permissions, and insurance policies; search for office space and purchase office furniture and equipment; draft brochures and other documents; and detail immediate program plans and service strategies.

To immediately get the board started on the right foot, a conscientious founder makes sure that proper governance procedures receive appropriate attention. If members of the founding board are unfamiliar with the roles and responsibilities of board service, it is crucial to set aside the time to study good practices for effective boards. Every board member should have an orientation to board service, liability issues, and roles and responsibilities of individual board members and boards as a collective group. Ensuring that recruitment of future board members is set in motion right from the start is simply smart planning. If outside experts are needed for these tasks, arrange for the board to meet with them. Forming a capable and responsible board from the beginning helps to secure the future of the organization and sets proper risk management processes in motion.

Prior to or at the beginning of the first meeting, identify who will be taking the meeting minutes. Besides divvying up the tasks during the first meeting, the board will need to set up a schedule for future meetings. Before the next full board meeting takes place, the minutes of the first meeting need to be ready for approval. These minutes will serve as the reference for the foundation of the board of this new nonprofit organization.

What Is the Purpose of an Annual Meeting?

Surprisingly, there seems to be considerable confusion about the necessity and purpose of annual meetings. An annual meeting refers to a meeting that every board of a nonprofit corporation must convene once a year in order to fill vacancies on the board, elect officers, and to approve any necessary actions to keep the organization and the board functioning. Unlike other meetings held throughout the year, the annual meeting is required by law.

In practical terms, an annual meeting forces the board to tend to necessary business on a regular basis. It does not mean that all compulsory issues must be squeezed into an annual meeting, but that all compulsory issues need *attention* and if this does not happen in one meeting, there must be additional meetings throughout the year.

If there are no vacancies, naturally this activity does not occur. However, sharing annual reports and financial statements, and approving a budget are other activities that the board must attend to. This item sharing and approval can take place during the annual meeting — as can any other usual business that requires attention.

Unless state law specifically stipulates when the annual meeting should take place, most annual meetings occur at the very beginning of the fiscal year. For example, if the fiscal year ends in December, it is common to have the annual meeting in January. This facilitates the tracking of terms for board members, allows the board to start the year with a new budget, and provides time for the chief executive to reflect on the past year's accomplishments.

See page 56 for additional discussions on annual meetings relating to membership organizations.

Special or Emergency Meetings: Taking Care of the Unforeseen

No matter how well the board predicts the future and foresees possible problems or otherwise unpredictable events lying ahead, it can never rule out the need for emergency or special meetings with certainty. On top of regularly scheduled meetings, there should be provisions for calling special meetings, the guidelines for which should be spelled out in the bylaws.

Emergency meetings may become necessary if suddenly the chief executive no longer can carry out the duty of managing the organization, a scandal is revealed in the media, or if there is a sudden change in the financial status of the organization. Any situation that requires the immediate attention of the board can warrant a special session. Other special meetings may not have a catastrophic undertone but still require the board to react before the next regular meeting. These situations may address serious constituents' complaints, time-sensitive approval of financial transactions, or handling of opportunities that would be missed if the board waited any longer.

The bylaws should indicate how to define a special meeting, who can call one to order, how much notice is required, how many board members need to be present, and how to share the decision with those board members who were not able to attend. It is important to eliminate the use of special meetings for deviant purposes — to use them in a manipulative manner to enforce decisions that would be difficult to obtain under normal circumstances. Some boards have executive committees empowered to take first action under emergency circumstances. Please see page 54 for more information on executive committee meetings.

COMMITTEE MEETINGS: THE BOARD'S WORKSHOP

There is hardly a board member who has not attended a committee or a task force meeting. In fact, most board work is accomplished through committees. Committees and task forces do the legwork for the board or digest comprehensive materials into a manageable format. (For a more complete discussion on committees and how they work, see the *BoardSource Committee Series* on page 79.) Committees come in all shapes and sizes; this influences the manner in which meetings are conducted. Communication differs whether there are three people in the room or 20. The more committee members, the more structure is needed in order to avoid possible chaos.

A committee is generally part of the overall board structure, has a specific charge, and may be stipulated in the bylaws, e.g., governance committee, executive commit- tee, and financial committees. A task force is organized to research a particular issue for later recommendation and debate by the board, or carry out a specific objective within a certain amount of time. Task forces are established on an as-needed basis, as opposed to standing committees, and allow for greater flexibility in the work of the board and its structure. An *action committee*, a committee that is primarily involved in the actual work of the organization (setting up special events, lobbying, making field visits), may not work in a meeting room at all but rather find themselves carry- ing out specific tasks in the field.

Committee leadership sets the tone of the meeting and an experienced facilitator can help produce positive results. The level of formality is often influenced by the preference of a committee chair. As there are no legal guidelines to determine how a committee must function, the leadership impacts the processes, involvement of members, and overall effectiveness of the group. Some meetings follow a strict order; others resemble more of a social gathering.

Whether a committee keeps minutes or not is up to the group to decide. Like any group assigned with a task, it makes sense to take notes. These notes may resemble standard minutes or they may be organized in any other coherent manner. As long as they serve the purpose of recording important group decisions and communicating the accomplishments of the session, they add value.

The minutes of a committee meeting are not the same as the committee report prepared for board review. The full board does not need to know how the committee meeting was structured but what the committee suggests for board action, what information the board must have at its disposal before it can proceed, and what other information is relevant for collective decision making. The report needs a format that eliminates unnecessary details and leaves behind a well-digested and comprehensive account of what the committee was to accomplish. If this issue is not clear to committee chairs, the board chair or the governance committee must ensure that proper education takes place.

Committees are charged with bringing recommendations to the board and cannot make organizational decisions, no matter how profound their conclusions. **The board is not obligated to follow the committee's suggestions.** It hopefully is able to assess the committee reports' validity and totality and, after that, proceed to make a final decision. A competent committee may have non–board members as expert advisors as well as board members in training who may provide out-of-the-ordinary questions and perspectives during discussion.

Equally, even if committee or task force members do not bear the same liability for their decisions as full-fledged board members, they are bound by the same ethical and moral standards. It is wise to ensure that committee volunteers are covered by the same directors' and officers' insurance that protects board members.

HOW DO BOARD MEETINGS DIFFER FROM COMMITTEE MEETINGS?

Issue	Board Meetings	Committee Meetings
Purpose	Make organizational and board-specific decisions	Draft recommendations for board action and carry out tasks assigned by the board
Composition	Elected board members (with a vote); advisors (nonvoting members)	Board members; former board members; outside experts or organizational members; volunteers
Frequency	Determined by need; legally must have an annual meeting; special meetings possible	Determined by scope and purpose of task
Accountability	Board works for the organization	Committees work for the board
Attendance	Required (duty of care)	Volunteer commitment to share work load
Liability	Decisions are legally binding; personal liability if members are not meeting duties of care and loyalty	Decisions are only recommendations; normally no collective or personal liability
Structure	Some parliamentary order is necessary; bylaws and policies define details	Determined by the committee chair
Reporting	Minutes are a legal document	Reporting is informational; no legal obligation exists

EXECUTIVE COMMITTEE MEETINGS:
ACTING ON BEHALF OF THE BOARD

If a board determines that an executive committee could be structurally and functionally helpful, the committee's role and limit of authority must be formally defined. The executive committee is the only standing committee that may make decisions on behalf of the board, even if the full board must subsequently confirm the decision during the next board meeting.

A carefully designed executive committee may serve different purposes, which in turn will determine the structure of the meetings. If the committee is there to act as a sounding board and overall support for the chief executive, the meetings may be carried on over the telephone. Burning issues determine the agenda. If the executive committee is the master coordinator of board work, the committee will likely meet regularly and work as the board's complexity mandates. If its task is to guide the board's focus, its meetings should be closely synchronized with board meetings. This type of executive committee works on the organization's priorities and strategic items and ensures that board meetings will not linger on administrative matters. If the executive committee's duty is to administer the performance evaluation of the chief executive, it should do exactly that, meeting with the full board afterwards to deliver the final assessment results. If the role is to act on behalf of the board under emergency conditions, the meetings may bring the committee members together without much preparation, or the meeting may take place over the phone and compel the members to use their best judgment without all the necessary background information.

Because of the variety of responsibilities that can be delegated to an executive committee, it is often impossible to plan a schedule ahead of time or anticipate when the committee *should* meet. This is a demand that executive committee members need to understand and accept.

In order to prevent the appearance of the executive committee as an exclusive "inner circle," **the executive committee should always keep meeting minutes.** If the committee makes decisions for the board, it must be able to document the circumstances of these decisions. The minutes must be distributed to every board member after the meeting. If the meeting consists of chatting with the chief executive, official minutes clearly are not necessary, but notes are. Notes serve as a record of the conversation and as a reminder of specific recommendations or points that need attention.

MAKING USE OF EXECUTIVE SESSIONS

An executive committee meeting and an executive session are not synonymous. As previously described, an executive committee is a standing committee of the board; an executive session is an exclusive meeting of the whole board behind closed doors — no staff, no guests, often no chief executive. Besides some executive committee meetings, if there is one meeting that tends to create anxiety, suspicion, and sense of secrecy, it is an executive session.

In spite of that, **every board can and should use executive sessions**. All boards have the right to meet without outsiders in the room. There are situations when the presence of staff, including the chief executive, or other nonmembers may hinder open deliberation. Some situations demand confidentiality and must be handled in privacy. Other circumstances simply allow board members to have a moment to share feelings and opinions about their respective relationships and their role vis-à-vis the organization.

WHEN IS AN EXECUTIVE SESSION NECESSARY?

The following circumstances may demand confidentiality, candid exchange of opinions, protection of individual rights, or need to improve board performance:

- Investigation of alleged improper conduct by a board member

- Discussion of financial issues with an auditor

- Preparation for a legal case with a lawyer

- Exploration of planning for major endeavors, such as mergers or real estate deals

- Discussion of the board's approach to a scandal or negative publicity

- Handling of personnel issues, such as chief executive compensation, performance evaluation, or disciplinary issues

- Handling of any other matters where confidentiality has been requested or is otherwise prudent

- Peer-to-peer discussions about board operations

There are also clear rules when an executive session is not in order. Boards should not revert to executive sessions for any of the following reasons: to avoid discussing tough issues in the open; to dodge responsibility; to restrict any board member's access to information by excluding him or her from a meeting; to purposefully create a secret society atmosphere and air of suspicion. The purpose of the session must be clear ahead of time and as soon as the issue has been handled, a regular meeting should proceed. The chair is responsible for calling these sessions and using them appropriately, but any board member may request one. Bylaws or board policies determine how to proceed.

Chief executives sometimes feel threatened by closed meetings from which they are excluded. For example: A chief executive was distressed when she realized that the board was suddenly meeting alone and barred her, specifically, from the room. Afterwards it became clear that the board wanted to plan the details for a special anniversary in her honor. To ease unnecessary worries, the board must communicate with the chief executive following the session and inform him or her of possible conclusions or recommendations that surfaced during the meeting. If the board holds these meetings on a regular basis — for instance, before or after each board meeting — suspicions can be dispelled. Trust and regular open communication will alleviate apprehension.

The minutes of the board meeting should indicate when the board has met in executive session. There should be a record of the purpose of the session, time and place, who was present, and a description of any actions taken. Sometimes these notes are mere annotations because the session simply helped the board to prepare for open discussion on a tricky item. These records should be shared with any or all participants afterwards. Executive session minutes or notes are not shared with outsiders, as that would betray the meeting's confidentiality.

CONVENING AN ORGANIZATION'S MEMBERSHIP

Any nonprofit that has a formal membership structure must also understand the legal rights of its members and for the membership's meetings. The source for these laws is the state nonprofit incorporation act. The Web site www.prairienet.org/~scruffy/f.htm can serve as a preliminary tool for research, but the office of the secretary of state or attorney general should also be able to provide the necessary information. State nonprofit associations also serve as an excellent reference for these issues.

State laws normally explain the processes for certain voting procedures and for sending out membership meeting notices. If quorum requirements are not detailed in the organization's bylaws, state laws will usually define these requirements (a common members' quorum is a mere 10 percent of the voting membership, but considerable deviation of this example exists).

A membership organization's annual meeting is usually not as confusing as one in an organization with a self-perpetuating board. Many associations and other membership nonprofits often have annual elections for new board members and the membership must be convened for this purpose. Most state laws allow proxy voting in membership meetings. This makes sense, as it is often impossible in large

---

WHAT IS A FORMAL MEMBERSHIP ORGANIZATION?

The term "member" can be very confusing and may have many different meanings:

- An organization may have a membership program that, for a fee, provides members with special benefits such as discounts, newsletters, or access to special Web site documents. In this context, the membership has no input into programmatic areas or the composition of the board — nor any other special affiliation with the nonprofit.

- A nonprofit may have members who are actually supporters of the mission and work of the organization. For instance, for a fee, members of a health-related organization may receive regular information on a particular illness, the latest research results, or suggestions for prevention and treatment. Again, the membership is not necessarily involved in the decisions that the board or the organization makes but members personally value its mission and work.

- A formal membership organization is one whose mission is to serve its members, such as a trade association, and one that invites its members to take an active role in the affairs of the nonprofit. The role of the members is outlined in the articles of incorporation and bylaws. Members usually elect the board and possibly also the officers of the board. They may also have the right to approve changes in the bylaws as well as major organizational decisions. Setting up a formal membership organization is a significant move and should not be taken lightly.

member organizations to gather all or even the majority of members in the same room at the same time. In addition to member attendance, voting can be done by mail or electronically. Most member voting issues turn out to be simple yes or no votes on prestated issues, or choosing a candidate from a slate. Communication with the membership prior to the meeting takes the role of deliberation of traditional board meetings, as proxy voting is a common method of participation. Membership meetings can also turn into heated debates, but in the end the objective is to reach a decision — particularly because reconvening the meeting at a later date can be costly and complex. If adequate and impartial information is shared with every voting member, it should be possible to conduct an unbiased election or receive a fair result of the members' opinion on an issue.

The bylaws should outline the chosen processes so that nobody needs to inquire about the state laws and wonder how and if a specific issue is covered. Additional details can be described in a policy manual, referencing membership meetings. Having an election committee in place ensures the reliability and trustworthiness of the voting process.

DUTIES OF AN ELECTION COMMITTEE

When ballots are used for voting at a membership meeting, a special election task force, or tellers, can ensure that proper process is respected. This committee or task force may have the following duties:

- Ensure legality of the process.

- Determine who can vote.

- Validate proxies.

- Prepare and distribute ballots.

- Collect and validate ballots.

- Provide a tally of the votes.

- Announce the results.

- Prepare a report.

To attract more members to the meeting, associations often organize their annual conferences at the same venue. In addition to attending conference activities, the membership also has the incentive of exercising its right to influence the internal affairs of the organization by electing a capable board and having an influence on the kinds of benefits offered by the organization.

RETREATS: HELPING TO GO FORWARD

Board retreats constitute a very special type of meeting. In some ways, they could be considered with *special meetings*, but because their structure and purpose is so different from a meeting where organizational decisions are made, they warrant a category of their own.

Retreats involve the board as a group. They are often used for purposes of education, training, reflection, planning, or socializing. A retreat brings board members (and frequently senior staff) together to provide an environment where free communication and brainstorming is possible. Often an outside facilitator is brought in to lead the proceedings to give every board member the opportunity to participate fully. Retreats can last from several hours to several days, often taking place over a weekend. Besides business, socializing usually plays an important role during retreats. This is an excellent opportunity to mix work and recreation in order to allow board members to get to know one another more intimately in a setting different from the more formal boardroom.

A retreat can be organized around a board orientation, a strategic planning session, a fundraising workshop, a board self-assessment, or a discussion of major internal or external strategic issues that are important to the nonprofit. If possible, the retreat should not take place in an office setting. A different environment helps send the message that new ideas and innovation are in order and creativity is desirable. There are a variety of special retreat accommodations to choose from and the board can be creative in selecting the location. A board can plan a retreat on a cruise ship, around a hiking tour or music festival, or other relevant events that tie the mission of the

---

TRY THIS!

During the next retreat, try one of the following ways to help the board generate ideas, brainstorm solutions, or address important issues.

Flipchart brainstorming — Using a flipchart, a large piece of butcher paper, or a chalk board, ask the board to generate a free-flowing list of ideas without censorship. Encourage freedom of thought and do not discuss suggestions as they are presented. Save the discussion until the end of the exercise.

Fishbone — This exercise is used to analyze cause and effect. On a large piece of paper, draw the head and the bones of a fish. Next to the head write down a problem. Label the backbone with a possible cause. As other causes surface add those to the side bones.

Mind mapping — Draw a circle on a big piece of paper and write a word inside, representing an issue. Draw lines off of the circle and label them with the various aspects of the issue. Add new lines with relating ideas as spokes off of the main lines.

Sticky notes — Ask each board member to write down individual ideas on separate pieces of sticky note paper and place them on the wall or in the middle of a table. Together, the board separates all ideas into similar categories and discusses the results.

Subgroups — Divide the group into smaller subgroups and ask each team to discuss either the same issue or separate issues and record their suggestions. Have a leader from each group present their findings to the main group.

organization to the board's focus. A good mixture of programmatic brainstorming activities and entertainment can help board members leave the retreat with a personal and professional sense of satisfaction and accomplishment.

Because of the nature of the meeting, retreats are rarely structured as normal board meetings. However, a retreat needs careful planning in order to ensure its success. It often makes sense to involve board members in retreat planning and organization. With ownership comes commitment. Retreats should be scheduled well ahead of time as busy board members need to manage their calendars, and travel and hotel accommodations may be involved. Spouses accompanying board members should be included in any social activities. The business side of the retreat, however, should not be open to family or friends.

The deliverables of a retreat depend on the purpose of the meeting. If the purpose was to discuss the results of a self-assessment, the board should produce an outline for future actions. A retreat focusing on strategic planning should include someone responsible for drafting the final document or taking the next steps. And the results of a retreat centered on better understanding of board members' roles and responsibilities will hopefully be evident at subsequent board meetings.

Boardroom Q & As

The following section is devoted to special board meeting dilemmas — situations with which many boards struggle and answers to questions that chairs, individual board members, or chief executives seek during their efforts to turn board meetings into the effective and productive events that they are meant to be. You can find guidance throughout the entire book, but these Q&As focus on specific common challenges and allow the reader to contemplate the recommended solutions.

Do not, however, accept these suggestions blindly. Use them with your board to help your board members become more innovative and seek new solutions to old problems.

Q: HOW CAN WE BRING ABSENT BOARD MEMBERS BACK TO THE MEETINGS?

A. Absenteeism needs a remedy. You must go to the root of the problem and for each individual case determine whether you are dealing with a personal dilemma or whether a change in the meeting structure or logistics can help the case. It is counter-productive to lump all missing team members in the same basket. Every board member has a personal relationship and connection with the board and the organization. By addressing the origin of each individual situation, you can try to bring change. The chair is the leader and motivator for board members and, in that capacity, usually is in the best position to propose solutions. Here are some steps you can take to bring missing board members back to the boardroom.

- Communicate to all new and established board members that attendance is obligatory.

- Make meetings matter. Spend time on the important issues.

- Use your board members. Give them meaningful roles.

- Listen to your board members' reasons for not coming to meetings before reprimanding them.

- If not evident, ask your members to suggest how obstacles for attendance may be removed.

- Have policies outlining a removal process when absenteeism becomes a problem.

Q: IS THERE AN IDEAL FREQUENCY FOR BOARD MEETINGS? IS THERE A COMPROMISE BETWEEN GETTING EVERYTHING DONE AND ULTIMATE BURNOUT?

A. When board members show signs of burnout and indicate that their workload is unreasonable, it is time to find the culprit for this condition. Ask the following questions to help isolate the reason or reasons for this work overload.

- Is our board big enough to accomplish all the necessary objectives?

- Are we going through a special transition that temporarily tests our capacity?

- Is our board doing board work or are we getting involved in operational issues that belong to staff or specific committees?

- Do we have an efficient committee and task force structure to help with the board's work?

- Have we tested different meeting frequencies and lengths of meetings?

- Are we efficient at getting our tasks accomplished?

Q: WHAT ARE OUR OPTIONS FOR MEETING EXPENSE REIMBURSEMENT FOR BOARD MEMBERS?

A. Particularly regional and national boards have a special challenge when recruiting new board members. The cost of coming to meetings may prevent some valuable candidates from joining your board. At the same time, transferring the financial burden to your organization is not necessarily the best or easiest solution. Here are possible options if you decide to adopt a meeting attendance reimbursement policy.

Option 1: No reimbursement. Your board members accept the personal responsibility to absorb all the costs.

Option 2: Reimburse upon request. Allow individual board members to determine whether they need reimbursement or are willing and able to pay all or part of their own expenses.

Option 3: Reimburse expenses. Set acceptable caps and standards to be able to control the overall cost. Include the expense cost item in your budget.

Q: OUR BOARD MEETING DISCUSSIONS SEEM DISORDERLY. HOW CAN WE LEARN TO STAY FOCUSED?

A. To keep your board focused on the right issues, you need some structure and an unwavering master of ceremonies. Some of the following tips might help the chair lead the discussion while not dampening the enthusiasm or exuberance of the fellow members.

- Install basic parliamentary principles if meeting procedure seems too unwieldy.

- Draft a clear agenda that functions as the roadmap for the meeting.

- Allot time frames for agenda items.

- Limit length of comments and number of times a board member may speak; assign someone as a timekeeper for every meeting.

- Provide focused material in the board packets that frames the issues in deliberate terms, helping to avoid sidetracks.

- If a fellow board member possesses particularly strong facilitator skills, it is perfectly acceptable to ask him or her to lead the discussion.

Q: How can we build more cohesion and agreement into our decision making and avoid split votes?

A. Diversity among board members often means that numerous points of view need to learn to live together and bear considerate results. Deliberate disconnection often originates from personality clashes and personal aspirations or ambitions. These expressions are symptoms of deeper problems on the board. This kind of a divide needs particular attention and must be solved. But there are still many other situations where an impasse is a regular obstacle during decision making and prevents the board from moving on after a vote. Try the following suggestions to work out a solution.

- Use committees and task forces to prepare the board for discussion on controversial issues.

- Send out committee materials and other support material in board packets and expect board members to have read them.

- Agree on objectives before starting the discussion to eliminate a possible preliminary stumbling block.

- Test different decision-making processes outlined earlier in this book.

- If time allows, table the issue, do more research, and come back to the next meeting with fresh ideas.

- Rely on the chair's final judgment if he or she votes to break a tie.

Q: How can we facilitate effective communication for our board members between meetings?

A. Electronic communication is your best option today. It is fast, saves money, and allows your board members to keep in contact between meetings with little effort. It eliminates unnecessary meetings and provides a convenient method to handle minor issues and obstacles without major physical displacement. Start by taking an inventory of your board members' electronic capacity. If your board members possess basic computer know-how, brainstorm together about how you can capitalize on this asset. Consider the following ideas.

- Turn your board manuals and board packets into electronic documents. Send updates as attachments to e-mails.

- Encourage each board member to share helpful Web sites and available documents with peers.

- Consider creating an intranet site where board documents can be stored safely and provide board members with easy access.

- Create an e-newsletter for regular communication between the chief executive and board members.

- Send minutes to all board members as e-mails for review and for possible comments.

- Follow the present evolution of state laws allowing board meetings to take place electronically. If your state is active on this issue, be prepared to take advantage of it occasionally by drafting your own guidelines.

Q: How should we handle conflicts of interest during our meeting?

A. Conflict of interest is a natural phenomenon in the boardroom. Proper management requires an understanding of its importance along with a clear communication to all board members. In addition, the board needs to install solid guidelines for dealing with eventual conflict situations, along with firm enforcement of these guidelines. Make sure that the following steps are part of your process.

- Draft a conflict-of-interest policy and share it with all board and staff members.

- Define insiders or disqualified members within the organization.

- Define instances that constitute a conflict of interest.

- Define situations that make board service undesirable for a recruit or for a present board member.

- Ask every board member to update his or her disclosure form annually.

- Expect every board member to recuse him- or herself from discussion when there is a conflict of interest. If the policy so requires, ask the member to leave the meeting during the discussion.

- Expect the chair to be familiar with board member disclosure forms and don't be afraid to remind a member of a possible conflict during a meeting if the member either does not recognize the conflict or has forgotten.

- Be consistent with enforcement.

Q. We want to include a short "Governance Moment" (a time during a meeting that focuses the board on a specific governance issue) on a timely or controversial topic or a tricky issue. What are some ideas for these discussions?

A. It is an excellent idea to incorporate into every meeting dedicated time that focuses your board members on issues, questions, or processes that are not yet well defined. These discussions can lead to a decision or may become clear that there is a need for further study. "Governance Moments" can provide an invigorating break during the meeting. Here are some suggested topics.

- What criteria should we use to include or exclude our customers or clients as board members?

- Should we use peer review as a tool to re-elect our officers?

- What do we think about sabbaticals for our chief executive?

- What should our policy be on accepting stocks as a contribution? Should we sell or keep them?

- Should our chief executive be a voting member of the board?

Q: What are the basic ground rules that we need to observe in order to run a laid-back meeting that is still legal and orderly?

A. Even if the state laws do not spell out the actual format or processes, board meetings can still benefit from some structure. Order in the boardroom does not prohibit a friendly, congenial, or even relaxed atmosphere. Ground rules can eliminate irregularities and the unfair treatment of some board members. Like with any protocol, ground rules take away ambiguity, embarrassment, and missteps in unclear situations. Below is a list of some of the key elements that provide structure to meetings.

- **Civility** — Start with politeness, professionalism, and respect for others. This is simple adult behavior that is the expected norm in every board meeting.

- **Chair** — If your meeting does not have someone chairing it, you will have a group of individuals managing themselves. Just try dealing with the cacophony that happens when everybody in the room is determined to make their point all at once! A skillful and unbiased facilitator manages the process, participants, and atmosphere.

- **Quorum** — The very first thing before starting is for the presiding officer or the secretary to determine whether you have enough qualified voting members present. If you do not have a quorum, the only practical decision you can make is to adjourn the meeting and determine when to continue.

- **Call to Order** — Every board meeting starts with a call to order. That is the official opening of the session when the business of the meeting begins. Whether you use the customary "The meeting will be in order" or another more colloquial phrase ultimately does not matter. Any discussion or decision is now part of the order of the meeting and the results will be recorded in the minutes. If you do not have an official start, you may have difficulties getting everybody's attention and, afterwards, you may wonder whether an issue was part of the meeting.

- **Motions** — When we talk about parliamentary order, we often erroneously equate that term with motions. Even if your board does not follow *strict* parliamentary rules — and there are arguments why that is not necessarily the best approach for many small nonprofit boards — relying on motions to present issues for consideration makes sense. A motion basically is a structured way of bringing up a point that you want the board to address. The chair has to grant you permission to speak, you say "I move that…," and state your proposal. Some complicated motions can be presented in a written resolution format ("Resolved, that…") but you still have to introduce them to the rest of the board. Using motions sets a tone for a business meeting where issues are introduced in an orderly fashion.

  The above is only a simplified introduction to motions. Flip through the pages of any guide on parliamentary law and you will find pages and pages dedicated to various kinds of motions, when to present them, who can do it, when they are out of order, and what possible exceptions exist. Unless your board is a true aficionado of detailed decorum, you probably do not need to get much more detailed with this topic.

- **Seconding** — If you introduce a motion, you will also need to have that motion seconded. This simply means that a peer will say "Second!" and indicate that your suggestion is valid for deliberation. If nobody speaks (you do not need permission for this quick exclamation) even after the chair invites you to do so, this motion is dead and will not be considered.

- **Deliberation** — Under most circumstances, it is impossible and imprudent to jump from seconding to voting. The major part of your meeting time should be spent on discussion, debate, argument, counterargument, and justifying opinions. These sections of the meeting are the bread-and-butter parts. Use them liberally and wisely.

- **Abstentions** — During the voting phase, you have members voting for and against but there may be some peers who decide that their only option is to abstain. Whatever the motivation, it means that this board member does not want to express his or her opinion on that particular issue. If there is no conflict of interest involved, a person abstaining needs to realize that his or her nonvote may prevent the majority from carrying the vote. An abstention may end up counting as a negative vote.

- **Adjournment** — A meeting starts with a call to order and ends with adjournment. By closing the meeting the chair indicates that all motions have been completed and that official business has been accomplished. The chair may simply say, "If there are no objections, the meeting will adjourn."

- **Minutes** — Recording the minutes of a meeting cannot be avoided. You may have a secretary of the board do this, or as is also common, have a staff member assigned to handle this task. The board has no choice in whether the minutes are kept, so keep them as clear, comprehensible, and unambiguous as possible.

The above points form the skeleton of desirable meeting processes. Define your meeting process philosophy and tie it to acceptable parliamentary guides. If your bylaws name a particular resource as your tool, make sure you follow the text exactly or that you define how this tool is to be applied. One way to rely on professional guides is to reserve their advice for insurmountable obstacles and during regular proceedings be as accommodating as possible. This provides some flexibility to your proceedings and allows your focus to be on results and not process.

Conclusion

At BoardSource, when we refer to processes and procedures, the saying goes: "Once you've seen one board, you've seen one board." And so it goes with board meetings. There is no sense in drafting step-by-step strict rules on how a board should operate during its meetings. Each board must find this through its own trial and error.

This book provides boards with options for contemplation. The best advice for running a meeting is to use common sense, know the legal framework, and be guided by the board's expectations. Design the processes and operating framework accordingly as they fit the board's culture, and simply act like reasonable adults with good will and passion.

If there are any messages to take away from this guide, remember the following three objectives: **Be flexible. Define the boundaries. Make meetings matter.**

It is the board that determines what works best. A board must work collectively, learn from each other, and teach each other — no matter how different the players are. Each board must figure out what processes bring the desired outcomes and then be brave enough to follow through, even if the means do not correspond to the traditional norms. Each board member must keep an open mind while adapting to team culture. Individuality is an asset in a board member, but it's the collective body that determines the course of action.

Flexibility does not imply that there are no boundaries. Board meetings must follow legal conventions, bylaws stipulations, ethical guidelines, and rules and protocol that define civil and considerate behavior. Without knowing what is acceptable, members can step out of line and compromise their intentions. Knowing the limitations eliminates ambiguity and provides fairness and integrity to the processes.

If board meetings do not focus on real, important, and relevant issues, they can be a waste of time. No matter how impeccable and considerate the processes are, if the board is working on the wrong issues, it is only perfecting the outer framework. The purpose of the board meeting is to bring board members together to steer the organization to its next level of potential. If the meeting time is spent on trivial issues, members will lose interest and feel unappreciated. By being strategic in planning the meetings' focus, this allows the board to stay one step ahead, be proactive, and productively advance the mission of the organization.

Appendix I

SAMPLE DOCUMENTS

SAMPLE MEETING AGENDAS

Sample 1

[Name of organization]
Board of Directors Meeting
Monday, September 15, 20XX
2000 Main Street, Suite 200
Our Town, VA 22222

A. Welcome and Chair's Remarks

B. Consent Agenda

- Approval of minutes of May 15, 20XX

- Approval of agenda

- Chief Executive's Report

- Treasurer's Report

- Committee Reports

C. Collaboration Proposal

D. New Program Developments

E. New Business

F. Adjournment

Sample 2

[Name of organization]
Board of Directors Meeting
Date: Monday, March 15, 20XX
Time: 6 p.m.
Location: 100 Main Street, Our Town, ME 01234

Agenda Items	Accountable	Purpose	Time
Welcome	Chair		5 min.
Introduction of new members	Chair	Information	5 min.
Consent agenda • Previous minutes • President's report • Committee reports • Leasing contract	Chair	Decision	1 min.
City contract proposal	Mike Murphy	Decision	15 min.
Summer program	Lisa Letts	Decision	15 min.
Relocation proposal	Mary Mann	Discussion	30 min.
Term limits	Becky Bowes	Discussion	20 min.
Adjournment	Chair		1 min.

Sample Ballots

Sample 1

Ballot for Election of Board Treasurer

Instructions: Vote for three candidates. Mark preferences by using 1 or 2, with 1 indicating your first choice. Do not give any tie votes. The candidate with the highest score is the next treasurer.

Candidates	Rating
Alvin Anderson	
Bertha Bowman	
Christy Cooper	
David Dotson	

Sample 2

Ballot for Officer Elections

Instructions: To vote, place an "X" in the square beside the name of the candidate of your choice.

Chair

☐ Mike Miller
☐ Mary Marvin

Treasurer

☐ Paula Parker
☐ Peter Piper

Sample Resolutions

Sample 1

Resolution for Relocating the Office

Resolved, that the headquarters of [name of organization] will be relocated in Peoria, Kansas, in June 20XX.

Sample 2

Resolution to Recognize the Service of a Long-Time Board Member [present this document as a letter]

Mary Michaels, you are a respected colleague and a valued friend. After more than a decade of service with us, we offer our profound thanks for your steadfast commitment to [name of organization] and your participation as a member of this board.

This resolution is passed by unanimous acclamation and entered into the official minutes of today's meeting of the board of directors.

Sample Proxy

The undersigned appoints _____ as my proxy, to vote on my behalf at the Annual Meeting of [name of association], on February 28, 20XX.

February 1, 20XX

Signature

Sample Committee Report Template

Date:
Committee:
Members present:

Type of report:

- Update

- Recommendation for board action

- Recommendation for a policy change

Outline of issues:

Background information/support materials:

Recommendation:

Sample Minutes Templates

Sample 1

[Name of organization]
Board of Directors Meeting
Minutes of [date]

The Board of directors of [name of organization] met on [date, time, place].

Attendance:
Members present:
Members absent:
Staff present:
Guests:

A. Consent agenda
    [Indicate if any of the items were removed from the consent agenda.]
    Action:

B. Issue
    Outline of discussion
    Action:

C. Issue
    Outline of discussion
    Action:

D. Issue
    Outline of discussion
    Action:

    Attachments

Sample 2 *(cont. on next page.)*

Board of Directors Meeting Minutes
[Name and address of the organization]
[Time and place of the meeting]

Present:
Absent:

(cont.)

Item	Actor	Action
Call to order	Sam Smith, chair	called meeting to order
Welcoming remarks	Sam Smith, chair	introduced new members [names]
Consent agenda	Lilly Litton James Jones	moved consent agenda to be approved seconded
City contract proposal	Mike Murphy Sherry Shannon James Jones Lisa Letts Full board	outlined the proposal (see attachment) moved to approve the contract seconded the motion objected due to reporting constraints voted, motion passed
Summer program	Lisa Letts Jane Jeffries Bill Blass Full board	introduced advanced plans for summer camp (see attachment) moved to approve the plan seconded voted, motion passed
Relocation proposal	Mary Mann Janis Johnston Dina Davies Full board	explained the need for relocation due to poor condition of the present building requested the formation of a task force to look into pros and cons seconded agreed to elect a task force; Lisa Letts requested a report for the next meeting
Term limits	Becky Bowes Dina Davies Full board Janis Johnston	outlined the present term limit structure of the board; suggested formation of a task force to study benchmark data seconded agreed to appoint a task force; Dina Davies requested a report for the next meeting seconded
Adjournment	Sam Smith, chair	adjourned the meeting at 7:45 p.m.

SAMPLE MEETING EVALUATION FORMS

Sample 1

Meeting Assessment

Issue	Yes	No	Suggestions
Meeting followed the agenda			
Agenda focused on future issues			
Meeting started and ended on time			
All board members were active participants			
Chair led the meeting with skill			

Sample 2

Meeting Assessment

Please comment if you do not agree with the following statements:

Board packet materials helped me prepare for this meeting.

Our meeting focused on the right issues that should be our board's concern.

We stayed on track and kept the mission as our guide.

We covered all the issues thoroughly and objectively.

I left the meeting knowing what I need to do next.

My additional suggestions to improve our board meetings:

Sample 3

Key Questions about Meetings

The following are some key questions designed to help board and staff prepare for board meetings and to focus on the right issues before, during, and after the meeting. These questions could be incorporated into meeting evaluations.

Before the meeting

- Are board members receiving board packets well in advance?

- Have board members read the material and provided appropriate feedback? Do they understand and agree with the inclusion of the issues in the agenda?

- Is the material presented in a concise and focused manner? Is it easy to understand the main points of the agenda or do the main points get buried in trivia?

During the meeting

- Is the chair an effective meeting facilitator?

- Is there something new and surprising happening at every meeting?

- Is the discussion focusing on the big issues or are debates about administrative and management-related details?

- Do board members feel well utilized and that they are able to contribute their skills and expertise?

- Do board members leave feeling as though they have learned something?

- Are board members respectful of the comments and contributions of fellow members? Are members in basic agreement of the main issues even if their approach may be different?

- Are meetings always in the same old boring place with the same old boring food?

After the meeting

- Did anything happen between the last meeting and the next one?

- Do board members feel as though they have wasted their time and nothing got accomplished?

- Did board members actually finish their tasks before the next meeting?

- Is anyone communicating with board members in between the meetings?

And the other underlying issues…

- Are board members genuinely interested in the mission of the organization?

- Are members worn out and tired of the commitment?

- Do members make wholehearted efforts to participate and collaborate?

- Do members come to every board meeting?

- Do members demonstrate an understanding of the issues?

SAMPLE CONTENTS OF A BOARD PACKET

Board packets should reach board members at least one week before the meeting. Their purpose is to allow board members to prepare properly for the meeting and to feel comfortable with the consent agenda items. The packet should/could contain

- Agenda
- Financial statements
- President's report
- Committee reports
- Any relevant background information for discussion items
- Update on the issues to be voted on
- Related newspaper articles
- Update on relevant legal issues affecting the organization
- Organization's newsletter

OUTLINE FOR AN ORIENTATION RETREAT

Sample One-Day Board Orientation Retreat

Location:	Redroof Hotel Conference Facilities
Time:	January 15, 20XX, 9:00 a.m. – 8:30 p.m.
Objectives:	To introduce new board members to the organization, fellow board members, and our board processes
9:00 a.m.	Breakfast
9:30	Welcoming remarks Introductions of board members, chief executive, facilitator Introduction to the organization Questions and answers
10:15	Presentation on board member responsibilities and role of the board Clarification of expectations Small group discussion
12:00 p.m.	Lunch
1:00	Introduction to teamwork; role playing
2:30	Coffee break
3:00	Presentation of board processes and structure Group discussion on how to share work
4:00	Fundraising challenges
4:30	Wrap-up Sharing of first impressions
5:00	Free time
6:00	Gathering at the lobby for drinks and dinner Guest speaker: How to make your board experience an exciting one

Appendix II

REFERENCES ON PARLIAMENTARY ORDER

1. *The Scott, Foresman Robert's Rules of Order, Newly Revised.* Harper Perennial, 1990. 706 pages. With over 700 pages of parliamentary order, this is the most widely used handbook on meeting procedures. It dissects meetings into most minute regulations and provides an answer to all questions concerning proper parliamentary order. Provides formality to meetings but can be used to solve disagreements during more informal meetings as well.

2. Sturgis, Alice F. *Standard Code of Parliamentary Procedure.* McGraw Hill, 2001. This updated guide resembles *Robert's Rules of Order* but is simpler to use for smaller nonprofits.

3. Tortorice, Donald A. *The Modern Rules of Order: A Guide for Conducting Business Meetings.* American Bar Association, 1999. 80 pages. This guidebook provides a modern, simplified procedure for meetings that promotes efficiency, decorum, and fairness within an easily adopted format. It is best suited for meetings where members focus more on content rather than procedure.

4. Oleck, Howard L. and Cami Green. *Parliamentary Law and Practice for Nonprofit Organizations.* ALI-ABA, 1991. 180 pages. This is a clearly outlined guide, which provides both explanations and discussion on various aspects of meeting procedures. It walks you through the mechanics of meetings, different motions, voting methods, nominations, and elections.

5. Keesey, Ray E. *Modern Parliamentary Procedure.* American Psychological Association, 1994. 143 pages. Keesey's method was originally created for the American Psychological Association. It is a simplified system promoting open participation and deliberation. A reduced order and structure guides the meeting.

6. Carver, John. *Carver Guide: Planning Better Board Meetings.* Jossey-Bass, 1997. 18 pages. John Carver describes an effective board meeting that follows the guidelines of Policy Governance.

7. Cochran, Alice Collier. *Roberta's Rules of Order.* Jossey-Bass, 2004. This guide introduces ultimate flexibility to board procedures. It advocates that each board creates its own meeting guidelines that best fit the board's culture and embrace democratic principles. Other features include introducing motions after the problem and possible solutions have been identified and using of concordance — substantial agreement — rather than majority rule or consensus.

8. www.parliamentarians.org
    The Web site of the National Association of Parliamentarians provides guidance and resources on meeting procedures.

9. www.parliamentaryprocedure.org
    The Web site of the American Institute of Parliamentarians includes documents on parliamentary issues and book references on parliamentary order.

Appendix III

GLOSSARY

Adopt: approve or accept a proposal by voting

Agenda: list of issues to be discussed in a meeting

Amend: modify or change a motion before it is voted on

Annual meeting: [usually] a legally required meeting where new board members and officers are elected

Ballot: blank piece of paper or a form used in secret voting

Carry: adopt or approve a motion

Chair: presiding officer during a board meeting

Conflict of interest: personal or professional interest that prevents a board member from making an unbiased decision

Consent agenda: portion of a meeting agenda where routine items are listed and voted on without further discussion

Deliberation: process of careful consideration and debate of issues to be voted on during a meeting

Election committee: committee responsible for the voting process (usually) during a membership meeting

Executive committee: standing board committee that has the power to act on behalf of the board

Executive session: special meeting of the board where usually no staff is present

KPAWN meeting: meeting between the board and the chief executive where the chief executive may openly discuss issues that "keep the president awake at night"

Minutes: legal record of the actions during a meeting

Motion: formal proposal for action during a meeting

Notice of meeting: message, usually written, to clarify the date and the place of the meeting, sent to every member who has the right to attend the meeting

Parliamentary order: rules and procedures for deliberative assemblies

Poll: census or survey method for voters to express their opinion

Private agenda: personal motivation and interest guiding decision making

Pro tem: for the time being; refers to a temporary chair of a meeting

Proxy: authorization of another person to vote or act on your behalf

Quorum: minimum number of members required present before business can be carried out

Rescind: cancel a previous decision

Resolution: longer or complicated motion that should be presented in a written format for board action

Retreat: brainstorming or action-oriented meeting

Robert's Rules of Order: leading manual of parliamentary order

Roll call: determination of who is present by reading the names of the members aloud

Secondary motion: motion that can be made while the primary motion is still pending on an issue that relates to business already under consideration

Seconding a motion: approval of a motion by another member during a meeting

Secretary: board officer traditionally responsible for keeping the minutes

Sunshine laws: state open meeting laws

Vice chair: board officer who usually chairs the meeting when the chair is not available

Voice vote: voting method for board members to indicate "yes" or "no"

Vote: formal expression of an opinion under consideration

Suggested Resources

Andringa, Robert C. and Ted W. Engstrom. *Nonprofit Board Answer Book: Practical Guidelines for Board Members and Chief Executives.* Washington, DC: BoardSource, 2001. BoardSource has created the next best thing to sitting down face to face with thousands of board members and chief executives! Our revised edition of the best-selling *Nonprofit Board Answer Book* is organized in an easy-to-follow question and answer format and covers almost every situation you're likely to encounter in non-profit board governance, from structuring a board for success to nurturing strategic alliances with other organizations. Also included are action steps, real-life examples, and worksheets.

Angelica, Marion Peters. *Resolving Conflict in Nonprofit Organizations.* St. Paul, MN: Amherst H. Wilder Foundation, 1999. The guide's eight-step process shows you how to spot conflicts, decide whether to intervene, uncover and deal with the true issues involved, and design and carry out a conflict-resolution process. Helpful worksheets, checklists, and conflict-resolution forms keep the process on track, with additional exercises for learning and practicing conflict-resolution skills.

BoardSource Committee Series. Six Books. Washington, DC: BoardSource, 2004. This series features an introductory publication, *Transforming Board Structure: Strategies for Committees and Task Forces*, that provides a fresh look at how boards can streamline the work of the full board. Included is a CD-ROM with customizable tools and worksheets that are helpful in job descriptions, interview questions, and policies appropriate to specific committees. Also included in the series are the following books: *Governance Committee, Executive Committee, Financial Committees, Development Committee,* and *Advisory Councils.* Learn about the most crucial committees of the board and how each committee is unique in operation and intent.

Dietel, William M. and Linda R. Dietel. *The Board Chair Handbook.* Washington, DC: BoardSource, 2001. This handbook provides a complete guide to the chair's roles and responsibilities, suggestions for developing board policies and procedures, recommendations for handling a variety of problems, and advice for cultivating talent for future board leadership. Also included is a CD-ROM containing sample meeting agendas and customizable letters for asking a board member for a gift, cultivating and recruiting prospective board members, inviting someone to join the board, and more.

Ernstthal, Henry L. "Deciding How to Decide." Association Management (Vol. 54), March 2002. Henry Ernstthal has developed a process to help determine who is supposed to be engaged in decision making within the nonprofit. This process can help veer off micromanagement as it guides appropriate issues away from the board and into the hands of the staff. A predetermined process of deciding how to decide can eliminate unnecessary friction among the various parties and avoid unnecessary unilateral action.

Futter, Victor, Judith A. Cion, and George W. Overton. *Nonprofit Governance and Management.* ASCS and ABA, 2002. A compilation of expert presentations to board structures and processes, this book is a classic tool for serious scholars. The text addresses organizational and operational issues, with numerous chapters touching on meetings and meeting-related issues.

Grace, Kay Sprinkel. *The Nonprofit Board's Role in Setting and Advancing the Mission.* Washington, DC: BoardSource, 2003. Is your board actively supporting and advancing your organization's mission? Learn how board members can contribute to the creation of mission as well as communicate the mission and purpose to the community. Discover how your board can partner with organizational staff to implement mission and supporting policies.

Hopkins, Bruce R. *Legal Responsibilities of Nonprofit Boards.* Washington, DC: BoardSource, 2003. All board members should understand their legal responsibilities, including when and how they can be held personally liable and what type of oversight they should provide. Discover the essential information that board members should know to protect themselves and their organization. Written in nontechnical language, this book provides legal concepts and definitions, as well as a detailed discussion on ethics.

Horton, Thomas R. "Groupthink in the Boardroom." *Directors & Boards*, Winter 2002. Tom Horton contemplates on the mystery of how being part of a group of cohorts can dim your individual thinking and take you with the crowd without posing pertinent questions. His thought: "Good boards encourage both coherence and dissent."

Hughes, Sandra R. *To Go Forward, Retreat! The Board Retreat Handbook.* Washington, DC: BoardSource, 1999. A board retreat is perhaps the best place to address some of an organization's challenging issues. Whether you are planning a retreat around board orientation, strategic planning, or board self-assessment, this book provides dos and don'ts of successful retreat planning. The text includes tips for icebreakers, seating arrangements, involving staff and guests, and getting input from participants in the planning process. Also included are a retreat checklist and preretreat planning questionnaires.

Iglis, Sue and Liz Weaver. "Designing Agendas to Reflect Board Roles and Responsibilities: Results of a Study." *Nonprofit Management & Leadership*, Fall 2000. A well-planned agenda guides the board to focus on strategic issues rather than spend time on administrative matters. A study shows the impact of structuring agendas according to defined board responsibilities: connecting board members to their roles, and leading chief executives to change their ways of presenting information to the board.

Ingram, Richard T. *Ten Basic Responsibilities of Nonprofit Boards.* Washington, DC: BoardSource, 2003. More than 150,000 board members have already discovered this #1 BoardSource bestseller. This newly revised edition explores the 10 core areas of board responsibility. Share with board members the basic responsibilities, including determining mission and purpose, ensuring effective planning, and participating in fundraising. You'll find that this is an ideal reference for drafting job descriptions, assessing board performance, and orienting board members on their responsibilities.

Katzenbach, Jon R. and Douglas K. Smith. "The Discipline of Virtual Teams." *Leader to Leader*, Fall 2001. This article studies how making virtual teams affects the teams' performance. Surprisingly, the authors conclude that technology as a tool is not the critical factor in performance — undisciplined behavior is. At the end, the authors recommend face-to-face sessions for problem solving and virtual meetings for information sharing and updates.

Kelsey, Dee and Pam Plumb. *Great Meetings! How to Facilitate Like a Pro*. Portland, ME: Hanson Park Press, 2001. *Great Meetings!* addresses challenges of meeting facilitation and provides practical tools, outlines, checklists, and options for handling group interaction and problem situations in the most productive manner possible. A facilitator will learn how to handle conflicts and when to intervene to make the best out of a tense situation.

McLaughlin, Thomas A. "Time to Work: No More Monthly Board Meetings." *The NonProfit Times*, October 1, 2001. How often a board needs to meet depends on the amount of work to be accomplished. Too-frequent meetings tend to encourage short-term thinking rather than enhance the board's supervisory capacity. A decision to meet less frequently should not happen in a vacuum, but careful analysis will help the board find the optimal number of meetings per year.

Orlikoff, James E. and Mary K. Totten. "Trustee Workbook: How to Run Effective Board Meetings." *Trustee*, April 2001. This article focuses on the main elements of effective meetings: keeping the board as the decision-making body, avoiding trivia in the agendas, ensuring the meetings are regularly evaluated for their efficiency, and bringing the right people into the boardroom.

Peterson, Mary. "Constructive Conflict." *Association Management*, August 2002. Conflict is a natural phenomenon; how we deal with it turns it into a negative or positive exchange. Peterson addresses honesty as one of the essential ingredients of conflict management. We also need to examine existing — written and unwritten — agreements between various participants to clarify expectations, she says. Actively dealing with conflict rather than avoiding it helps to keep the situation under control and not allow it to escalate into a major confrontation.

Pointer, Dennis and James E. Orlikoff. *The High-Performance Board: Principles of Nonprofit Organization Governance*. San Francisco: Jossey-Bass, 2002. Sixty-four principles outline the critical areas that the board must pay attention to. The authors provide recommendations for each aspect of board focus and develop an action plan for continuous board education.

Robinson, Maureen. *Nonprofit Boards That Work*. New York: John Wiley & Sons, 2001. Maureen Robinson acknowledges that there is no unique formula that meets the needs of every board. The board's desire to do the best for the organization takes many forms. There is a solution to every situation and the author provokes each board to find its own application. The board must assume flexibility and adaptability to become a board that works.

Schwarz, Roger M. *The Skilled Facilitator: Practical Wisdom for Developing Effective Groups*. San Francisco: Jossey-Bass, 1994. A professional facilitator finds this book as the authoritative guide to ground rules of group interaction, proven techniques for starting a meeting and keeping it focused, practical methods for dealing with emotions that hinder progress, and a diagnostic tool to identifying problem areas.

Sunshine laws: www.rcfp.org/tapping/index.cgi. This Web site provides direct access to the various state sunshine laws.

Susskind, Lawrence, Sarah McKearnan, and Jennifer Thomas-Larmer. *The Consensus Building Handbook*. Thousand Oaks, CA: Sage Publications, 1999. Here is the most comprehensive resource on consensus building. Over 1,100 pages explain and document best practices in the consensus-building discipline. Experts in the field outline their methods to solve problems and make decisions in a group setting, and 17 case studies demonstrate how facilitators and mediators have relied on consensus-building principles.

Tesdahl, D. Benson. *The Nonprofit Board's Guide to Bylaws: Creating a Framework for Effective Governance*. Washington, DC: BoardSource, 2003. It is important that your board periodically review and adjust its bylaws in response to organizational change and growth. This newly revised book will help your board determine how your organization is best structured, the rights of the participants within the structure, and important organizational procedures. Included in the text are findings from a BoardSource- conducted survey, providing recent empirical data about how nonprofits handle certain issues. Don't miss the sample bylaws provisions and the conflicts-of-interest policies on the accompanying diskette!

Waldenmayer, Corinne. "Connecting a Far-flung Board." *The Grantsmanship Center Magazine*, Fall 2002. National and international boards often struggle with distance-related obstacles to bring all board members together under the same roof. Technology-based tools connect remote regions and enable these boards to function. This article introduces options and helps organizations decide which ones are worth the investment.

Zander, Alvin. *Making Boards Effective: The Dynamics of Nonprofit Governing Boards*. San Francisco: Jossey-Bass, 1993. This hardcover book remains the classic resource on interpersonal dynamics of boards. It tells a valid story of how individual board members' characteristics and the processes that the board chooses to employ affect the overall performance of the board. Understanding causes and effects of human behavior and the absence of committed decision making can lead to self-serving and rubber-stamping boards.

About the Author

Outi Flynn, Director of the Knowledge Center at BoardSource, has been part of staff since 1989. For the past several years she has developed, structured, and managed the Board Information Center, one of the most highly utilized and popular services BoardSource has offered.

Outi has created and contributed to the bulk of the governance information available on BoardSource's Web site, including topic papers and frequently asked questions, and acts as the primary content reviewer for the organization's publications. Her areas of expertise cover overall sector issues, dilemmas that concern nonprofit leaders on a daily basis, and structural and procedural challenges that affect board productivity.

Outi holds a bachelor's degree in nutrition from Framingham State College.